Applied Marketing Science / Angewandte Marketingforschung

The book series "Applied Marketing Science / Angewandte Marketingforschung" is designated to the transfer of top-end scientific knowledge to interested practitioners. Books from this series are focused – but not limited – to the field of Marketing Channels, Retailing, Network Relationships, Sales Management, Brand Management, Consumer Marketing and Relationship Marketing / Management. The industrial focus lies primarily on the service industry, consumer goods industry and the textile / apparelindustry. The issues in this series are either edited books or monographs. Books are either in German or English language; other languages are possible upon request.

Book volumes published in the series "Applied Marketing Science / Angewandte Marketingforschung" will primarily be aimed at interested managers, academics and students of marketing. The works will not be written especially for teaching purposes. However, individual volumes may serve as material for marketing courses, upper-level MBA- or Ph.D.-courses in particular.

Sören Köcher

The Paradox of Points

Theoretical Foundation and Empirical Evidence of Medium Magnitude Effects in Loyalty Programs

With a foreword by Prof. Dr. Hartmut H. Holzmüller

Springer Gabler

Sören Köcher
Dortmund, Germany

Doctoral Dissertation, TU Dortmund University, 2014

Applied Marketing Science / Angewandte Marketingforschung
ISBN 978-3-658-09542-0 ISBN 978-3-658-09543-7 (eBook)
DOI 10.1007/978-3-658-09543-7

Library of Congress Control Number: 2015936081

Springer Gabler

Printed on acid-free paper

Springer Gabler is a brand of Springer Fachmedien Wiesbaden
Springer Fachmedien Wiesbaden is part of Springer Science+Business Media
(www.springer.com)

To Sarah

Foreword

Loyalty programs have become one of the most important instruments for improving customer retention. A fundamental common principle among these programs is that they offer their members a certain number of units of a program currency such as frequent flyer miles, loyalty points, or stamps on the basis of cumulative spending on the provider's products or services which, in turn, can be exchanged for rewards. However, despite this similarity loyalty programs in business practices widely differ regarding the magnitude of their program currency. This dissertation focuses on the effects stemming from these medium magnitudes on customer-provider relationships.

More precisely, within his thesis Sören Köcher systematically investigates the effects of the magnitude of loyalty program currencies on the central consumer decisions in a loyalty program membership; namely, participation, redemption, purchase, and reward decisions. The results of twelve empirical studies discover a seemingly paradoxical finding: High magnitude currencies improve the attractiveness of collecting units of the program currency but entail reluctant spending behavior. In addition, this dissertation examines under which conditions theses effects appear and vanish. Despite the abundance of previous academic research on loyalty schemes the investigation of the effects of alleged irrelevant variations of the magnitude of loyalty program currencies on consumer choices remain unexplored. Hence, this monograph enhances our comprehension of how loyalty program currencies work and, therefore, is of very high scientific as well as practical relevance. From a theoretical perspective, this research discovers a contradiction of one of the most fundamental principles of rational choice theory and, thus, contributes to a better understanding of when and why people deviate from rational decision-making. In addition, since variations of the magnitude of loyalty program currencies have to be considered as cost neutral, the implications resulting from the findings of this dissertation should be of particular interest for companies planning to develop and implement loyalty programs as well as for firms which already launched a loyalty scheme.

With his work, Sören Köcher impressively demonstrates his expertise and skills regarding experimental research and associated methods of analysis. The documented studies are composed, conducted, and analyzed in a very purposeful, creative, and comprehensive manner. Aside from the methodological quality, this dissertation is based on a very solid presentation of conceptual and theoretical background knowledge. The author provides a concise, up-to-date literature review of previous research on loyalty programs and individual choice behavior. In addition, he succeeds in discussing and reflecting his empirical results against existing theories but also in advancing the discipline's theoretical knowledge.

In sum, this dissertation truly expands our understanding of how loyalty program currencies influence consumer choice behavior to a large extent and provides significant theoretical contributions as well as valuable managerial implications for improving the performance of such programs in business practices. Thus, I hope and wish that this book and its insights will enjoy a wide readership and high acceptance among academics as well as practitioners.

Dortmund, January 2015 Prof. Dr. Harmut H. Holzmüller

Acknowledgements

Many friendly, smart, and generous people have supported my dissertation project in one way or another. First and foremost, I want to express my sincere gratitude to my dissertation supervisor, Prof. Dr. Hartmut H. Holzmüller. I greatly appreciate his support, encouragement, and faith in me and my work. He gave me the freedom to pursue my own ideas and, at the same time, the guidance I needed during the writing of my thesis. The experience I gained through his generous support helped me to grow both professionally and personally. I could not imagine a better environment for conducting doctoral research than the one he provided for me. Furthermore, I thank Prof. Dr. Andreas Engelen for his readiness to be the second examiner of my thesis. My gratitude also goes to the third member of the dissertation committee, Prof. Dr. Stefanie Paluch. Aside from providing valuable advice, she motivated me to work on additional projects and helped me get in touch with the scientific community by way of many joint conference contributions. I truly enjoyed our collaboration and our conversations on topics academic and otherwise.

I owe special thanks to Prof. Dr. Markus Blut for piquing my interest in experimental research as a young academic, and for his kind encouragement of my first research efforts. In addition, I want to thank my former and current colleagues and team members at the Department of Marketing of TU Dortmund University for hints, insights, and valuable suggestions on and off topic. I thank Nicole Ahl-Saelbstaedt, Gerrit Cziehso, Christoph Dotterweich, David Egbert, Alexander Eiting, Ulya Faupel, Debra Hanning, Vanessa Haselhoff, Sabrina Heix, Lars Jensen, Isabelle Kes, Andreas Kessenbrock, Florian Kopshoff, Christian Martin, Fabian Pahl, Lena Reimers, Stefan Ruffer, Sugiththa Sabaratnam, Christian Samulewicz, Jun.-Prof. Dr. Tobias Schäfers, Catharina Spliethoff, Laura Teichmann, Alke Töllner, Jasmin Ulrich, and Moritz vom Hofe. Furthermore, I thank our student assistants, who carefully kept track of my library loans and brought my plants back to life.

Many people outside of academia also contributed to the completion of this book. I thank my friends for their constant encouragement and support in every respect. I would like to single out Florian for helping in proofreading the final manuscript although he is probably the busiest person I know. I am grateful to my parents who did a multitude of things to help me reach this point. My mother, however, deserves more thanks than I could ever give. She always had faith in me, was proud of me, and took care of me. She did everything in her power to support me throughout my entire life, and I am forever thankful for that.

Finally, I want to express my deepest gratitude to Sarah. I am grateful for your love and patience, your steadfast belief in me, and your support, as well as for your understanding during the countless hours I spent in front of the computer screen. I thank you for being by my side no matter what, for offering me calm during stressful times, as well as for your unlimited willingness to read my manuscripts and to rehearse the thesis defense presentation again and again and again and again. I would not have been able to overcome the challenges I have encountered during the past years without a place where I can feel at home; this place is where you are.

Dortmund, January 2015 Sören Köcher

Table of Contents

List of Figures

List of Tables

A Introduction

"[T]he potential implication of research on medium is not medium; it is extra large."

(Hsee et al. 2003, p. 1)

1 Motivation and Purpose

Today, loyalty programs are ubiquitous. Since American Airlines launched the first program of its kind in 1981, loyalty schemes have incredibly spread and now cover various industries, including retailing, travel and hospitality, as well as financial services. In particular, the recognition that customer retention strategies are less costly than customer acquisition efforts (e.g., Demoulin and Zidda 2009; Heskett, Sasser, and Schlesinger 1997; Lal and Bell 2003) and that customer loyalty has a positive impact on a firm's long-term financial performance (e.g., Anderson, Fornell, and Lehmann 1994; Reichheld and Sasser 1990; Reichheld and Teal 1996) can be held responsible that many companies endow these relationship programs with utmost importance. As a result, the world's ten leading hotel chains, nine of the ten biggest airlines, and eight of the ten largest retailers in the United States run loyalty schemes.

Despite their apparent underlying motivation to induce loyal purchase patterns, customers are surprisingly fascinated by these programs. More than 71 million people around the world collect frequent flyer miles offered by American Airlines' loyalty program AAdvantage (InsideFlyer.com 2013), whereas about 77 million customers of Intercontinental Hotels participate in the IHG Rewards Club, the world's largest hotel chain program (IHG.com 2013). In 2013, more than 50 percent of German households were enrolled in Payback, Germany's biggest reward program with approximately 600 cooperating program partners, and collected points worth €186 million (LoyaltyPartner.com 2014). Although over 30 years have passed since the launch of the first loyalty scheme, they still feature stunning growth rates. For instance, a recent study found that loyalty program memberships in the United States increased by 26.7 percent from 2010 to 2012, reaching a total of 2.65 billion enrollments (Berry 2013).

One common theme among these programs is that they offer their members a certain number of units of a program medium (Bagchi and Li 2011; Hsee, Zhang, and Zhang 2003; van Osselaer, Alba, and Manchanda 2004) such as frequent flyer miles, loyalty points, or stamps based on cumulative spending on the program provider's products or services which, in turn, can be used to redeem a reward, e.g., free products, cash-backs, or other gifts (e.g., Lemon and von Wangenheim 2008; Liu 2007; Smith and Sparks 2009). While most programs fall back to this simple reward mechanism, they vary in terms of the magnitude of their program currency. For instance, an airline may either decide to set up a program which offers 1 point per flight and a free flight for 10 points or a program with 100 points per flight and a free ticket for 1,000 points. Although the exchange rates between trips and points, respectively points and rewards, differ, these differences caused by the magnitude of the program medium should be irrelevant as both programs require exactly the same effort (10 paid tickets) for the same outcome (a free ticket). Nonetheless, behavioral choice theories suggest that this might not always be the case.

Given the great popularity of loyalty programs on both sides, companies and customers, it is hardly surprising that a broad body of literature has been devoted to acquire insights into diverse aspects of this relationship instrument (see Dorotic, Bijmolt, and Verhoef 2012 for an extensive review). Numerous studies concentrate on the effectiveness of loyalty programs by investigating the relationship between program participation and loyal behavioral patterns (e.g., Bolton, Kannan, and Bramlett 2000; Lal and Bell 2003; Mägi 2003). Furthermore, various studies have examined to what extent loyalty program design (e.g., De Wulf et al. 2003; Kivetz and Simonson 2002; Nunes and Drèze 2006a) and customer characteristics (e.g., Gómez, Arranz, and Cillán 2012; Liu 2007; van Doorn, Verhoef, and Bijmolt 2007), as well as environmental factors (e.g., Liu and Yang 2009; Meyer-Waarden 2007; Wright and Sparks 1999) drive consumer behavior. However, despite the abundance of literature on loyalty schemes the investigation of the effects of medium characteristics received only limited attention. Although previous research highlights that alleged irrelevant variations of program medium specifications influence customers' perceptions of loyalty programs (Bagchi and Li 2011) and even purchase patterns (e.g., Kivetz, Urminsky, and Zheng 2006; Nunes and Drèze 2006a; van Osselaer et al. 2004), the effects of medium magnitude on consumer choices in a loyalty program membership remain unexplored. Thus, the purpose of this dissertation is to bridge this gap and improve our knowledge of medium magnitude effects in loyalty programs by conceptually and empirically establishing a comprehensive framework centered on their impact on the central consumer decisions in loyalty program memberships. In addition, to provide deeper insights into when and why these effects appear, boundary conditions will be identified.

The contribution of this thesis is of equal relevance from both perspectives, managerial as well as theoretical. First, although advanced technologies facilitate the maintenance of loyalty schemes (e.g., Deighton 2000; Sopanen 1996), developing and operating such programs are still considered as a costly investment of money and effort (e.g., Bolton et al. 2000; Lal and Bell 2003; Smith and Sparks 2009) whose effectiveness reflected in changes of established behaviors has often been questioned (e.g., Dowling and Uncles 1997; Henderson, Beck, and Palmatier 2011). This research provides a better understanding for a more efficient usage of loyalty programs in business practices by offering essential findings about how program members' decisions are affected by a program currency's magnitude. Second, from a theoretical perspective, this dissertation yields new insights as to when and why different presentations of consequentially equivalent choice problems entail diverging decisions and, thereby, discovers a violation of one of the most fundamental assumptions of rational choice theory causing deviations from rational decision-making.

2 Structure of the Thesis

The purposeful examination of medium magnitude effects in loyalty programs in this thesis is subdivided into five parts organized as follows: Following this introductory *part A*, *part B* provides the conceptual basis for this dissertation. It comprises a holistic definition of loyalty programs and an examination of their key elements. The subsequent literature review structures extant research on loyalty programs by identifying four key decision fields in loyalty program memberships—namely, participation, redemption, purchase, and reward decisions—and summarizes central findings within each decision context. In addition, the basic concept of medium magnitude effects is exposed and related phenomena are discussed.

The first section of *part C* reviews the relevant theoretical background for this thesis. This section provides a fundamental explanation of rational choice theory and its essential underlying assumptions as well as an outline of three descriptive approaches. Based on this overview of theories, in the second section, a research model comprising medium magnitude effects within each of the identified decision fields is developed. Besides direct effects, the proposed hypotheses also refer to boundary conditions of the influence of medium magnitude on consumer choices. Finally, the empirical approach centered toward testing the hypothesized effects is presented.

The empirical investigation of the impact of medium magnitude on customer decisions is documented in *part D*. To provide solid evidence for the proposed effects, each of the four key decision fields is subject to three studies varying among contexts, data collection methods, sample structures, and statistical methods of analysis. Thereby, each study series systematically examines the main effects of medium magnitude as well as their boundary conditions.

Finally, conclusions from the examination of medium magnitude effects in loyalty programs are drawn in *part E*. It contains a summary of the major findings of the empirical investigation, a discussion of theoretical contributions to different streams of literature, and recommendations for business practices. A critical review of limitations and directions for further research concludes this dissertation. Figure 1 summarizes the outlined structure.

Figure 1. Structure of the Thesis

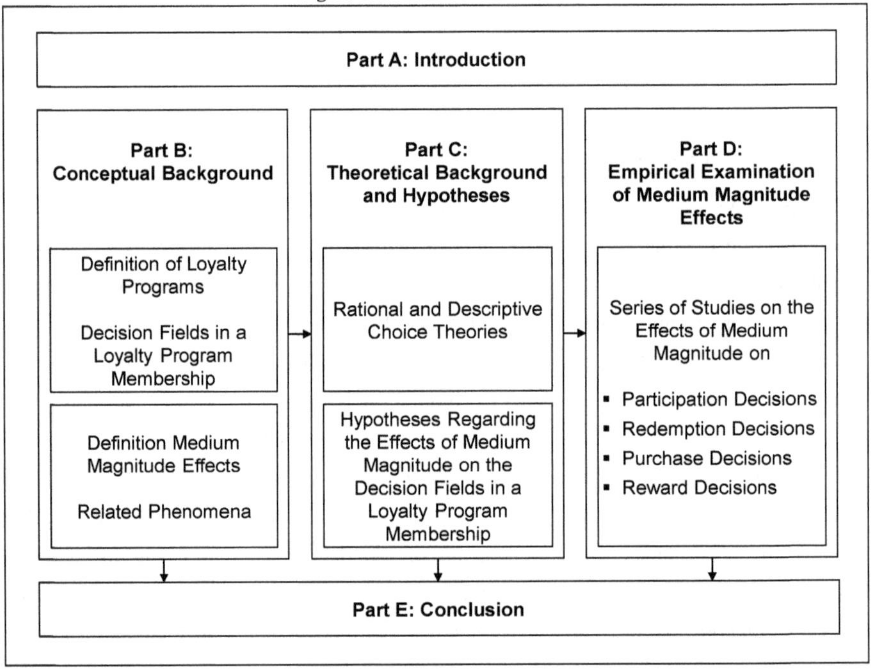

B Conceptual Basis and Literature Review

This section provides the conceptual foundation for this thesis. Chapter 1 gives a brief description of loyalty programs and its associated key elements. Next, chapter 2 reviews and discusses previous research on consumer decisions in loyalty program memberships. Finally, in chapter 3, the basic idea of the central concept of this dissertation, namely, medium magnitude effects in loyalty programs, is introduced and related phenomena are described.

1 Loyalty Programs

Building on extant loyalty program literature the following sections outline the concept of loyalty programs. This outline includes the development of a holistic definition of this concept which incorporates its key elements. Subsequently, these elements are described in more detail.

1.1 Definition

Loyalty programs can take many forms. In practice, program schemes differ greatly in terms of membership requirements, the number of partnering companies, types and values of rewards offered, as well as medium collection and redemption mechanisms. Some merely focus on a specific product category, others reward purchases of all products and services at a wide range of companies; some programs offer cash-backs and discounts to engage customers in loyal behaviors, whereas others incent program members with special treatments. However, despite the abundance of different loyalty schemes in business practices and various different terms to describe such programs (e.g., reward, frequency, continuity, or affinity programs), there seems to be a consensus among extant academic literature about the concept of loyalty programs and its fundamental elements.

Table 1 gives an overview of selected definitions whose similarities provide the basis for the following discussion of the key elements of loyalty programs. A closer look at this collection of definitions confirms a consistent understanding of loyalty programs and identifies four frequently recurring themes; namely, development and enhancement of loyalty, reward function, program structure, and long-term orientation (see also Dorotic et al. 2012).

Table 1. Selected Definitions of Loyalty Programs

Author(s)	Definition	Key Elements
Dowling and Uncles (1997, p. 71)	"Loyalty programs […] seek to bond customers to a company or its products and services by offering an additional incentive […]."	Development of Loyalty, Reward Function
Henderson et al. (2011, p. 258)	"[…] we define a loyalty program as any institutionalized incentive system that attempts to enhance consumers' consumption behavior over time […]."	Enhancement of Loyalty, Program Structure, Reward Function, Long-Term Orientation
Kim, Shi, and Srinivasan (2001, p. 99)	"Reward programs, a promotional tool to develop customer loyalty, offer incentives to consumers on the basis of cumulative purchases of a given product or service from a firm."	Development of Loyalty, Reward Function, Program Structure
Lal and Bell (2003, p. 179)	"These programs offer various incentives and rewards to consumers on the basis of cumulative purchases from a given provider, be it a store, a service, or a manufacturer."	Reward Function, Program Structure
Lewis (2004, p. 281)	"Such programs encourage repeat buying and thereby improve retention rates by providing incentives for customers to purchase more frequently and in larger volumes."	Enhancement of Loyalty, Reward Function
Liu (2007, p. 20)	"A 'loyalty program' is defined as a program that allows consumers to accumulate free rewards when they make repeated purchases with a firm. Such a program rarely benefits consumers in one purchase but is intended to foster customer loyalty over time."	Reward Function, Program Structure, Enhancement of Loyalty, Long-Term Orientation
Liu and Yang (2009, p. 94)	"We define loyalty programs as long-term-oriented programs that allow consumers to accumulate some form of program currency, which can be redeemed later for free rewards."	Long-Term Orientation, Program Structure, Reward Function
Meyer-Waarden (2007, p. 224)	"Loyalty programs, which represent tools for developing relationships and SOW, offer integrated systems of marketing actions and economic, psychological, and sociological rewards."	Development of Loyalty, Reward Function
Noble, Esmark, and Noble (2014, p. 361)	"Loyalty programs offer customers benefits in exchange for repeat patronage to an organization."	Reward Function
Rayner (1996, p. 8)	"A customer loyalty scheme is a mechanism for identifying and rewarding loyal customers."	Reward Function, Program Structure
Sharp and Sharp (1997, p. 474)	"Loyalty programs are structured marketing efforts which reward, and therefore encourage, loyal behaviour."	Program Structure, Reward Function, Development of Loyalty
Yi and Jeon (2003, p. 230)	"A loyalty program is a marketing program that is designed to build customer loyalty by providing incentives to profitable customers."	Development of Loyalty, Reward Function

First, the fundamental objective of loyalty programs is to develop and enhance attitudinal or behavioral loyalty and, thus, to realize the economic benefit of long-term business relationships. Hence, loyalty programs should encourage existing customers to maintain or increase their purchase amounts and frequencies (e.g., Dowling and Uncles 1997; Sharp and Sharp 1997; Strauss, Schmidt, and Schoeler 2005). The second common thread among loyalty programs is that they recognize and reward their members for their loyalty by providing tangible or intangible incentives in return for repeat business (e.g., Dowling and Uncles 1997; Kivetz and Simonson 2002; Meyer-Waarden 2008). This reward function, in turn, might serve as reinforcment that encourages consumers to maintain their rewarded purchase patterns or even increase their purchase volumes through concentrating as much of their business as possible on one seller (e.g., Keh and Lee 2006; Long and Schiffmann 2000; Taylor and Neslin 2005). Third, loyalty programs follow a defined structure. They are typically membership-based such that, first of all, customers have to sign up to participate (Dorotic et al. 2012). At their most basic, program members then collect some kind of program currency (i.e. program medium) based on their purchase volumes and frequencies which can be exchanged for rewards after reaching a minimal redemption threshold (e.g., Carlsson and Löfgren 2006; Leenheer et al. 2007; Noble et al. 2014; Sharp and Sharp 1997; Wright and Sparks 1999). Thus, besides program requirements, the key specifications of a loyalty program structure include thorough definitions of the medium issuance and redemption mechanisms (Liu and Yang 2009). Fourth, loyalty programs are long-term oriented, as they are explicitly intended to foster loyal behaviors over time. This characteristic separates loyalty programs from other short-term promotional activities which do not create comparable lock-in effects (Liu 2007; Sharp and Sharp 1997). Hence, loyalty programs constitute a long-term investment for both the company and its customers (Dorotic et al. 2012; Liu 2007).

In conclusion, the majority of the compiled definitions of loyalty programs predominantly failed to meet all of the above outlined elements and, hence, might be incomplete (see table 1). Therefore, in this dissertation:

> *Loyalty programs are defined as long-term oriented relationship instruments intended to develop and enhance customer loyalty by rewarding and, thus, encouraging program members' loyal purchase patterns according to a well-defined program structure.*

1.2 Key Elements of Loyalty Programs

The following sections discuss the identified program elements—i.e., development and enhancement of customer loyalty, reward function, program structure, and long-term orientation—more precisely.

1.2.1 Development and Enhancement of Customer Loyalty

While the specifics of loyalty schemes widely differ, the core motivation for companies to employ this relationship instrument is to build and increase customer loyalty (e.g., Henderson et al. 2011; Liu 2007; Yi and Jeon 2003) which is reflected in steady or increasing retention and repeat-purchase rates, customer lifetime durations, shares of requirements, purchase frequencies and volumes, as well as higher degrees of cross-buying behavior (e.g., Dowling and Uncles 1997; Lal and Bell 2003; Lewis 2004; Mägi 2003;). Hence, loyalty programs as part of a defensive marketing strategy (Sharp and Sharp 1997) focus on retaining (profitable) existing customers (e.g., Bolton et al. 2000; Kumar and Shah 2004; Lewis 2004) and stimulate their purchase behavior (Meyer-Waarden 2007)—as opposed to acquiring new customers (Noordhoff, Pauwels, and Odekerken-Schröder 2004). Extant research suggests three underlying mechanisms to be conducive to a program's effectiveness in terms of the formation of loyal purchase patterns; namely, the creation of switching costs (e.g., Kim et al. 2001; Kopalle and Neslin 2003; Wirtz, Mattila, and Lwin 2007), generation and utilization of consumer insights (e.g., Graeff and Harmon 2002; Mauri 2003), and reduced intensity of competition (e.g., Kim, Shi, and Srinivasan 1997; Kopalle and Neslin 2003; Lal and Bell 2003; see figure 2). These factors are discussed more detailed subsequently.

Figure 2. Underlying Mechanisms of Loyalty Program Effectiveness

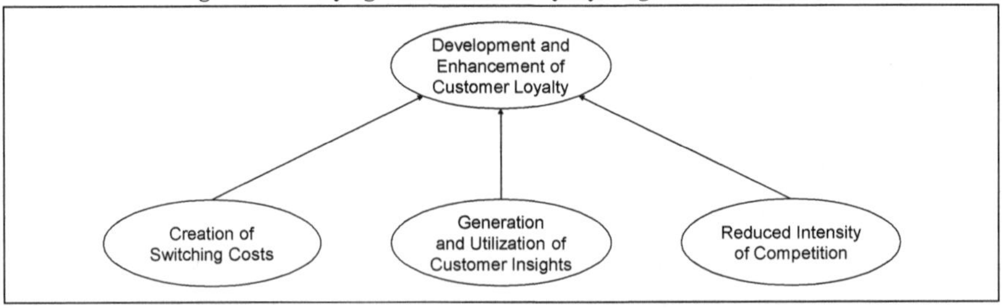

1.2.1.1 Creation of Switching Costs

Loyalty programs can foster customer loyalty by creating different types of switching barriers (e.g., Bolton et al. 2000; Carlsson and Löfgren 2006; Kim et al. 2001; Kopalle and Neslin 2003; von Wangenheim and Bayón 2007) including financial, relational, and procedural switching costs (Burnham, Frels, and Mahajan 2003). First, loyalty program members are locked in since switching providers may imply a loss of accumulated benefits. For instance, program currencies in terms of miles or points accrued through past purchase actions are typically not transferable to another firm (Drèze and Hoch 1998; Meyer-Waarden 2008; Sharp and Sharp 1997; Wirtz et al. 2007; Zhang, Krishna, and Dhar 2000). As the level of rewards usually depends on the length of the relationship between a customer and the focal company, changing providers produces a significant time lag before similar rewards can be obtained from another firm (Verhoef 2003). Second, loyalty programs can create relational switching costs which additionally strengthen lock-in effects (Meyer-Waarden 2007). Customers may appreciate provided rewards giving them a feeling of preferential treatment and a sense of belonging (Dowling and Uncles 1997) reflected in increased levels of commitment and trust toward the company (Morgan and Hunt 1994). Finally, switching providers may also involve procedural costs in terms of expending time and effort, when joining another company's loyalty scheme, to learn its program structure (Wirtz et al. 2007).

1.2.1.2 Generation and Utilization of Customer Insights

Furthermore, loyalty programs enable marketers to collect valuable consumer data (Graeff and Harmon 2002; Mauri 2003; Nunes and Drèze 2006b) and, thus, to acquire and enrich knowledge about their customers (Leenheer and Bijmolt 2008). This customer information, typically comprising personal data—primarily obtained through an initial enrollment process (e.g., Wansink 2003)—and transaction data—gathered through recording of purchases (e.g., Kumar and Shah 2004)—allows the employment of advanced marketing techniques. These techniques, including precise targeting of profitable customers and customer segments (Ashely et al. 2011; Demoulin and Zidda 2009; Hansen, Deitz, and Morgan 2010) via direct, personal, customized or segment-specific communication and offerings aspired toward meeting heterogeneous customer needs (Wansink 2003; Meyer-Waarden 2008; Lacey and Sneath 2006), increase the profitability of marketing actions (Dowling and Uncles 1997) and enhance the ability to build long-term customer relationships (Wansink 2003; Mauri 2003). Besides, these consumer insights can be harnessed for improving promotions, product and pricing policies, as well as optimizing category management (Cortiñas, Elorz, and Múgica 2008; Lacey and Sneath 2006).

1.2.1.3 Reduced Intensity of Competition

Finally, loyalty programs can help companies to elude competition. Especially in highly competitive markets with limited opportunities to differentiate from competing providers (e.g., grocery and petrol retailing), the implementation of a loyalty program might be an effective strategy to develop a point of uniqueness (Kumar and Rao 2003; Wright and Sparks 1999). However, such a differentiation is often difficult to maintain in the long run, as competitive reactions in the form of imitations might neutralize the value of a single loyalty program (Dowling and Uncles, 1997; Dowling, Uncles, and Hammond 2003; Kopalle and Neslin 2003; Leenheer et al. 2007).

In addition, loyalty schemes might be an appropriate tool to mitigate the intensity of competition by counter-acting new and potential entrants by establishing barriers of market entry (Carlsson and Löfgren 2006; Kopalle and Neslin 2003; Liston-Heyes 2002). Moreover, loyalty programs can soften price competition through the creation of switching costs (e.g., Kim et al. 2001; Klemperer 1987; Lal and Bell 2003; Liston-Heyes 2002) and by solving oversupply problems during seasons of low demand (Kim et al. 1997; Noordhoff et al. 2004).

1.2.2 Reward Function

The second common theme among loyalty programs is that they reward their members for repeated purchases of the focal company's products or services. Psychological research has shown that rewards can be highly motivating (see Latham and Locke 1991 for a review) and, thus, it is reasonable to assume that during participation in a loyalty program, a customer might be disposed to respond to program benefits as intended (Roehm, Pullins, and Roehm 2002). In addition, rewards might be perceived as the firm's appreciation and personal recognition of its customers (Liu 2007) and function as a positive reinforcement to continue rewarded behavioral patterns (e.g., Sheth and Parvatiyar 1995; Taylor and Neslin 2005).

Program rewards are typically classified into economic (e.g., monetary advantages) and non-economic rewards (e.g., emotional, social, or psychological rewards; Demoulin and Zidda

2009; Drèze and Nunes 2009; Leenheer et al. 2007; Noble et al. 2014). Economic rewards, on the one hand, are financial benefits including cash-back rewards, free products or services, discounts, or savings (Arbore and Estes 2013; Demoulin and Zidda 2009; Jang and Mattila 2005; Lal and Bell 2003). However, these incentives are often criticized for being rather easy to imitate by competing firms and programs as well as for attracting price sensitive customers who lack brand loyalty (O'Malley 1998; Phillips-Melancon, Noble, and Noble 2011).

Non-economic rewards, on the other hand, are those benefits that lead to perceptions of belonging, special treatment, and personalized attention such as special privileges, restricted check-in counters, and priority on waiting lists (Arbore and Estes 2013; Dowling and Uncles 1997; Drèze and Nunes 2009; O'Brien and Jones 1995; Phillips-Melancon et al. 2011; Rosenbaum, Ostrom, and Kuntze 2005). This sense of being important—e.g., stimulated through establishing a hierarchy among the company's customers based on spending levels (e.g., Drèze and Nunes 2009; von Wangenheim and Bayón 2007)—can enhance customers' emotional connection to the firm (Bitner 1995; Gwinner, Gremler, and Bitner 1998) and is expected to be more effective in improving customer loyalty than economic rewards (Rosenbaum et al. 2005). An important aspect regarding program members' perception of status is the decision about the number of status levels and the relative size of each tier (Arbore and Estes 2013; Drèze and Nunes 2009; Kopalle et al. 2007). In this context, previous research has shown that—depending on perceptions of branch exclusivity (e.g., airlines versus supermarkets; Arbore and Estes 2013)—three-tier programs (e.g., gold, silver, no status) are more suitable than two-tier programs (e.g., gold and no status; Drèze and Nunes 2009). However, it should be noted that the segment of high-status customers reacts more sensitively to negative events such as denied service due to overbooking than lower-status customer groups (von Wangenheim and Bayón 2007).

In addition, rewards can be distinguished according to their timing in terms of immediate versus delayed rewards (Demoulin and Zidda 2009; Jang and Mattila 2005; Keh and Lee 2006; Noble et al. 2014; Roehm and Roehm 2011; Soman 1998; Zhang et al. 2000). Immediate rewards can be seen as price discounts offered at the time of subscription or for every visit, whereas delayed rewards are incentives that typically require the accumulation of multiple purchases and, hence, pursue to build exit barriers (Keh and Lee 2006; Yi and Jeon 2003). Accordingly, it has been found that immediate benefits are effective in getting consumers to switch away from competing brands, while delayed incentives foster customer retention through the creation of switching costs by rewarding their future purchases (Kim et al. 2001; Leenheer et al. 2007; Zhang et al. 2000).

Loyalty program benefits also differ regarding their congruence with the company's products and services. A company can either provide direct rewards (i.e. incentives that are closely related to company's products or services) or indirect rewards (i.e. benefits with no linkage with the company's offering; Demoulin and Zidda 2009; Dowling and Uncles 1997; Keh and Lee 2006; Kivetz 2005; Roehm et al. 2002; Yi and Jeon 2003). In terms of their cost efficiency, indirect rewards, in particular cash rewards, are deemed cost inefficient as the consumers' valuation of the reward equals the firm's cost of the reward. In contrast, direct rewards such as a free product of the firm are declared cost efficient incentives as the value to the customer exceeds the reward's cost (Kim et al. 2001).

Finally, the classification of rewards can be further refined by the distinction between luxury and necessity incentives (Jang and Mattila 2005; Kivetz and Simonson 2002), tangible and intangible rewards (Drèze and Nunes 2009; Roehm et al. 2002), as well as between stochastic (i.e. entries into lotteries with uncertain large rewards) and deterministic (i.e. smaller guaranteed rewards) rewards (Kivetz 2003).

Aside from the described types of incentives, loyalty schemes vary among the value of rewards (Kim et al. 2001; Kopalle and Neslin 2003; O'Brien and Jones 1995; Roehm and Roehm 2011; Soman 1998) and their variety (Drèze and Nunes 2007; Kumar and Shah 2004; O'Brien and Jones 1995), which both are influential drivers of the attractiveness and, thereby, effectiveness of loyalty programs (Roehm and Roehm 2011).

1.2.3 Program Structure

Loyalty programs are also similar in that they reward customers according to a predefined program structure. This structure includes specifications of membership requirements, the medium issuance and redemption mechanism, as well as the extent to which the program provider cooperates with partnering companies which also credit and redeem the program currency.

1.2.3.1 Membership Requirements

As the implementation of a loyalty program is accompanied by a discrimination of the customer base between members and non-members (Lacey and Sneath 2006; Leenheer 2004; van Heerde and Bijmolt 2005), the specification of the terms and conditions of participation constitutes a crucial program structure parameter. The registration for a program can be conducted voluntary by the company's customers or automatically by the company itself (Liu and Yang 2009). In this regard, the degree to which program enrollment is restricted to specific customer groups—i.e. participation exclusivity (De Wulf et al. 2003)—has to be specified (Leenheer 2004). Following O'Brien and Jones (1995), opening loyalty programs to a wide range of participants might involve a waste of resources in over-satisfying less profitable customers, while under-satisfying more valuable customers.

In addition, from a customers' perspective, program enrollment can require economic (e.g., membership-fees; Bolton et al. 2000; Kivetz and Simonson 2002; Liu and Yang 2009) as well as non-economic costs in terms of the amount of disclosed personal information through registration and subsequent identification at transactions (Leenheer et al. 2007); often resulting in a perceived loss of privacy (Ashley et al. 2011; Noble and Phillips 2004; van Doorn et al. 2007). Depending on the type and amount of collected data different types of card technologies are employed (see Worthington and Hallsworth 1999 for an overview).

1.2.3.2 Medium Issuance Mechanism

For a loyalty program to be effective, it should have a structure that enables customers to perceive purchases as a sequence of related rather than independent single transactions (Lewis 2004). Therefore, loyalty programs usually issue some kind of a program medium to their members at the time of purchase; typically depending on the monetary amount spent on the company (e.g., one point per dollar) or on the number of purchased products independent of their price (e.g., one point per coffee; Leenheer et al. 2007; Wright and Sparks 1999). Although program medium units have no value themselves until they are redeemed (Hsee et al. 2003; Rothschild and Gaidis 1981), their accumulation creates an anticipation of positive future benefits which increases consumers' likelihood of staying in the relationship (Lemon, White, and Winer 2002; Liu 2007). Despite their apparent similarity, medium issuance mechanisms in practice differ regarding several details. By way of illustration, table 2 provides an overview of exemplary medium issuance structures of selected hotel loyalty programs.

Table 2. Selected Hotel Loyalty Programs

Hotel Chain (Loyalty Program)	Medium Issuance	Redemption Threshold (free nights)	Status Levels and Point Bonuses	New Member Enrollment Bonus
Carlson Rezidor Hotel Group (Club Carlson)	$1 = 20 pts.	9,000 pts.	Silver (15 nights, 25%), Gold (35 nights, 50%), Concierge (75 nights, 75%)	2,000 pts.
Hilton (Hhonors)	$1 = 10 pts.	5,000 pts.	Silver (10 nights, 15%), Gold (40 nights, 25%), Diamond (60 nights, 50%)	-
Hyatt (Gold Passport)	1$ = 5 pts.	5,000 pts.	Platinum (15 nights, 15%), Diamond (50 nights, 30%)	-
InterContinental Hotels Group (IHG Rewards Club)	$1 = 10 pts.	10,000 pts.	Gold (15 nights, 10%), Platinum (50 nights, 50%)	3,000 pts.
Marriott (Marriott Rewards)	$1 = 10 pts.	7,500 pts.	Silver (10 nights, 20%), Gold (50 nights, 25%), Platinum (75 nights, 50%)	-
Starwood (Preferred Guest)	1$ = 2 pts.	2,000 pts.	Gold (25 nights, 50%), Platinum (50 nights, 50%)	-

First, the program currencies employed by the hotel chains vary among their magnitude which has an impact on the number of medium units credited for every purchase (e.g., 2 points at Starwood hotels versus 5 points at Hyatt hotels per dollar spent on the company) and, consequently, on the number of points required for redemption (e.g., 2,000 points for a free night at Starwood hotels versus 5,000 points at Hyatt hotels; see also Bagchi and Lee 2011). Second, all illustrated loyalty schemes are characterized by a non-linear medium issuance structure such that the number of earned points per dollar increases as a function of repeat purchase (Leenheer 2004; Hsee et al. 2003; van Osselaer et al. 2004). For instance, after staying 10 nights at a Hilton hotel, program members are promoted to silver status which qualifies them to earn 15 percent more points per dollar spent than basic members. Such ascending point schedules increase switching costs and, thus, enhance customers' motivation for continued business with the firm (Carlsson and Löfgren 2006). Besides the described convex medium issuance mechanism, the number of earned points as a function of accumulated spending can take a simple linear or even a concave shape (van Osselaer et al. 2004). Finally, two of the outlined issuance structures provide new members an enrollment bonus (i.e. endowed points at the time of subscription). Such a head start has been shown to have a motivating effect by improving program members' perceptions of progress toward a reward even if redemption thresholds increase by the number of initially endowed points (Kivetz et al. 2006; Nunes and Drèze 2006a; Zhang and Huang 2010).

1.2.3.3 Medium Redemption Mechanism

The medium redemption mechanism refers to the conditions for the exchange of medium units into rewards. In analogy to the medium schedule in the issuance context, the medium structure in the redemption stage can derive from a linear system (Carlsson and Löfgren 2006; Drèze and Hoch 1998; Hsee et al. 2003). Table 3 illustrates such a non-linear redemption structure by means of Lufthansa's frequent flyer program.

Table 3. Selected Flight Rewards of Lufthansa's Miles & More Program[1]

Destination (Departure Frankfurt, Germany)	Distance (in Miles)	Ticket Price (in €)	Ticket Price (in Bonus Miles)	Value per Bonus Mile (in €)	Value per Bonus Mile (in Miles)
Berlin, Germany	263	131	25,000	.005	.011
Rom, Italy	600	208	30,000	.007	.020
Beirut, Lebanon	1,762	536	40,000	.013	.044
Washington, USA	5,092	850	60,000	.014	.085
Mexico City, Mexico	5,949	1,059	70,000	.015	.085
Jakarta, Indonesia	6,906	1,322	80,000	.017	.086
Wellington, New Zealand	11,531	2,142	100,000	.021	.115

For instance, redeeming 25,000 bonus miles for a flight reward (e.g., a round-trip ticket for the flight route Frankfurt – Berlin) entails a monetary value of each redeemed mile of €.005—given a regular ticket price of €131—and a travel distance of .011 miles per bonus mile. In contrast, redeeming a flight reward requiring 100,000 bonus miles (e.g., a round-trip ticket for the flight route Frankfurt – Wellington with a regular price of €2,142) increases the monetary value of

1 Prices were retrieved on Februar 9, 2014 for departures on July 1st and return flights on July 6th 2014 (Lufthansa.com 2014).

each redeemed bonus mile by the factor four to €.021 and the covered distance by the factor ten to .115 miles per bonus mile. Hence, in this exemplary redemption structure both the monetary value as well the possible reach of a single bonus mile rise as a function of the number of redeemed bonus miles. Since such a non-linear redemption mechanism heightens the attractiveness of upscale rewards, it is expected to create similar switching costs as well as associated lock-in effects as non-linear medium issuance structures (Carlsson and Löfgren 2006).

Another important aspect in this context is the specification of redemption thresholds reflected in the number of accumulated purchases required for reward attainment (Drèze and Nunes 2011; Lewis 2004; Liu and Yang 2009; O'Brien and Jones 1995). On the one hand, a high redemption threshold may seem as unattainable and, thus, demotivate program members. On the other hand, if thresholds are particularly low, a program might not be challenging enough and may fail to engage customers (Drèze and Nunes 2011). In addition, as the specification of redemption thresholds is directly related to a program's cost, cost-effectiveness should be taken into account when deciding on the requisite number of purchases to obtain a reward (Wansink 2003). Furthermore, redemption systems in practice differ regarding the payment of rewards. Besides traditional single-currency pricing (e.g., 100 points for a free ticket), some loyalty programs in practice allow their members to combine points with cash to pay for rewards (e.g., 80 points + $20 for a free ticket; Drèze and Nunes 2004; Nunes and Drèze 2006b; Nunes and Park 2003). Regarding the effects of these payment mechanisms, Drèze and Nunes (2004) argued that a mixture of currencies lowers perceived costs to customers as the summation of both pricing components to total costs is biased. Finally, another redemption related aspect worth noting is the degree to which redemption policies are restricting reward redemption ranging from highly controlling (e.g., expiration terms and blackout dates) to not controlling (e.g., 10% off any item, anytime; Dholakia 2006; Noble et al. 2014; Phillips-Melancon et al. 2011). Strict reward policies might make members feel as if their autonomy or competence is restricted, whereas flexible policies foster feelings of freedom and autonomy (Phillips-Melancon et al. 2011). However, perceptions of these restrictions also depend on whether the offered rewards are social or economic in nature (Noble et al. 2014).

1.2.3.4 Program Partners

In addition to being rewarded for purchases of the offerings of a single company hosting the loyalty scheme, program partnerships exist such that participants can earn and spend the program currency by making purchases and receiving rewards from multiple cooperating firms (De Wulf et al. 2003; Lemon and von Wangenheim 2008; Sharp and Sharp 1997). For instance, the American Airlines Advantage Program contains more than 1,000 participating companies in diverse branches such as other airlines, hotels, financial services, retailers, and charities (aa.com 2014). Hence, another important characteristic of loyalty program structure is the extent to which a provider expands its program and cooperates with partnering companies. Considering multi-partner programs from a customers' perspective, as a consequence of their wider application—when compared to single-vendor programs—they are typically more attractive (De Wulf et al. 2003; O'Brian and Jones 1995; Wright and Sparks 1999). Besides, multi-partner schemes entail promising benefits for cooperating firms. Program partners can profit from each other's reputation through spill-over effects as well as customer cross-buying behavior (Lemon and von Wangenheim 2008; Meyer-Waarden and Benavent 2006). However, multi-partner programs might entail merely minor improvements regarding loyal purchase patterns for each participating company since they motivate their members to allocate their purchases among multiple firms rather than to concentrate them on a particular company (Sharp and Sharp 1997).

1.2.4 Long-Term Orientation

Long-term orientation, the fourth common thread among loyalty programs, highlights that loyalty schemes operate differently from other marketing techniques. For instance, due to their degree of defensive and long-term orientation, loyalty programs can be distinguished from sales promotions and advertising campaigns which are characterized by a clear time line and, accordingly, pursue distinct objectives (Sharp and Sharp 1997). These promotions aim to increase market share through a substantial gain in penetration and a small increase in average purchase frequency (Ehrenberg, Goodhardt, and Barwise 1990). However, when promotions finish, consumers tend to revert to previous purchase patterns (Ehrenberg, Hammond, and Goodhardt 1994). In contrast, continuous loyalty programs rarely pay off after one purchase but are rather intended to foster customer loyalty over time (Liu 2007). Hence, as opposed to promotion activities, they aim to gain more business from existing customers reflected in an increase of repeat-purchases without an increase in the number of customers (Sharp and Sharp 1997). Thus, these programs require a firm's long-term commitment as well as the customers' willingness to engage into a long-term relationship with the company (Reinartz and Kumar 2003).

2 Consumer Decision Fields in a Loyalty Program Membership

The study of loyalty programs enjoys great popularity. A broad body of literature deals with an investigation of this relationship instrument from diverse perspectives. Against the background of this dissertation—centered toward an examination of the effects of medium magnitude on consumer choice behavior—a classification of previous studies according to the decision context under consideration is developed.

A closer look at extant research on loyalty programs identifies four decision fields within a program membership, namely participation decisions (see chapter 2.1), redemption decisions (see chapter 2.2), purchase decisions (see chapter 2.3), and reward decisions (see chapter 2.4). The following sections state the nature of each decision field and review the main research findings on determining factors in each of these decision contexts. Chapter 2.5 concludes this literature review with a summarizing synthesis.

2.1 Participation Decisions

Since customers who refuse to join a loyalty program elude its intended effects, the customers' decision to become program member reflects the necessary condition to achieve the program related objectives. Hence, companies usually try to maximize the number of program participants to achieve the pursued objectives within a wide range of customers and, thus, to increase program effectiveness (Demoulin and Zidda 2009). From a customers' perspective, the decision to join a loyalty program is mainly determined by an assessment of the potential benefits of a membership relative to its costs (De Wulf et al. 2003; Kivetz and Simonson 2003; Leenheer et al. 2007; Noble and Phillips 2004; O'Brien and Jones 1995; Soman 1998).

Accordingly, previous research has demonstrated that the enrollment decision mainly depends on the customers' perceived level of effort—i.e. any inconvenience determined by the program requirements during participation (Kivetz and Simonson 2003)—to obtain program benefits—i.e. any reward members get in return for their participation (De Wulf et al. 2003). For instance, using a conjoint analytical approach, De Wulf et al. (2003) explored how different levels of consumer inputs (personal data release, participation cost, purchase frequency, participation exclusivity, and participation efforts) and outcomes (program benefits, number of program providers, and program duration) affect participation decisions. Their results confirmed that consumers, when deciding whether or not to join a program, aim to minimize their inputs, while maximizing expected outcomes. In addition, the program attributes of participation costs and program benefits drove consumers' intentions to participate for almost 70 percent; degrading remaining program attributes to minor relevance.

With regards to program benefits, Peterson (1995) revealed by means of qualitative interviews that both economic and social incentives are the main reasons to sign up. In a similar vein, Noble and Phillips (2004) exposed benefit-related barriers—caused through hollow, unknown, and unenticing rewards—that deter customers from enrolling in loyalty programs. A wide range of additional studies has highlighted the crucial role of economic benefits (e.g., Jang and Mattila 2005; Leenheer 2004; Leenheer et al. 2007; Wright and Sparks 1999) and non-economic rewards (e.g., Ashley et al. 2011; Demoulin and Zidda 2009; Leenheer 2004; Leenheer et al. 2007) in participation decisions.

Extant research on program efforts has focused on the effects of speed and ease of reward attainment (Jang and Mattila 2005; Kivetz and Simonson 2002, 2003), store distance (Allaway, Berkowitz, and D'Souza 2003; Demoulin and Zidda 2009; Kivetz and Simonson 2003), and previous purchase frequency (Ashley et al. 2011; Demoulin and Zidda 2009). In this context, a low shopping frequency has been found to be one of the major reasons to refuse program enrollment (e.g., Noble and Phillips 2004; Toh, Rivers, and Glenn 1991; Wright and Sparks 1999). Vice versa, heavy buyers who can easily benefit from a loyalty program membership without considerably changing their purchase behavior exhibit a strong motivation to participate (Demoulin and Zidda 2009; Kivetz and Simonson 2003). Moreover, inconvenience of registration (Ashley et al. 2011; Toh et al. 1991; Wright and Sparks 1999) and identification (Jang and Mattila 2005; Noble and Phillips 2004), as well as loss of flexibility in product, brand, or store choice (Toh et al. 1991; Wendlandt and Schrader 2007) constitute additional dimensions of program effort. Interestingly, Kivetz and Simonson (2003) showed in a series of experiments in diverse contexts (e.g., gas station, grocery store, and credit card programs) that individuals do not merely assess their own program-related effort per se to make their enrollment decision rather than compare their required investments to referent others—i.e. the effort of typical consumers—such that the likelihood of joining a loyalty scheme increases with effort advantage even if the absolute level of effort increases. Again, this perceived effort advantage can be driven by consumers' purchase frequency. In addition, Nunes and Drèze (2006a) indicated that reframing requisite efforts through endowed progress—e.g., offering enrollment bonus points when joining the program and simultaneously increasing the number of purchases required to redeem a reward—enhances the enrollment likelihood.

Furthermore, as customers who enter a loyalty program usually have to provide personal data, privacy concerns constitute a key parameter restraining program adoption (Ashley et al. 2011; De Wulf et al. 2003; Gómez et al. 2012; Leenheer 2004; Leenheer et al. 2007; Noble and Phillips 2004; van Doorn et al. 2007). The provision of such information and an associated perceived loss of control over personal data conduces to customers' worry about possible misuse or being targeted for direct mailings and other promotional activities (Graeff and Harmon 2002; Jang and Mattila 2005; Noble and Phillips 2004).

In addition, enrollment decisions are affected by customers' socio-demographic characteristics. The number of loyalty program memberships increases with income and the number of household members. Gender is a key discriminator when analyzing program participation; women tend to keep more memberships than men. Besides, persons aged between 35 and 64 show higher program participation rates than customers in age groups below or above (Liston-Heyes 2002; van Doorn et al. 2007; Wright and Sparks 1999). Other personal characteristics affecting the intention to participate include general attitude toward loyalty programs, desire for variety, and shopping enjoyment (Gómez et al. 2012).

Finally, when considering participation decisions, it is important to recognize that loyalty programs do not operate in an isolated environment such that their adoption not only depends on the customers' expected benefits and costs of a program itself but also on the existence and attractiveness of competing programs. However, findings on this factor are mixed. Whereas some researchers (Leenheer 2004; Wright and Sparks 1999) have confirmed a plausible negative impact of the number of memberships on the probability of joining further programs, others have shown a positive relationship between previous and future program adoption (Demoulin and Zidda 2009; Leenheer et al. 2007; Liston-Heyes 2002).

In conclusion, the above considerations suggest that program design elements (e.g., type and attainability of rewards) in combination with individual-level requirements (e.g., store distance and required change in purchase behavior) as well as personal attitudes (e.g., attitude toward loyalty programs), preferences (e.g., desire for freedom in product, brand, and store choice) and socio-demographic characteristics (e.g., gender, income, and age) determine the customers' expected program benefits and costs and, thus, the decision whether or not to join in a loyalty scheme. Table 4 provides an overview of empirical studies on participation decisions.

Table 4. Summary of Research on Participation Decisions

Author(s)	Study Description	Major Findings
Allaway et al. (2003)	Scanner data analysis in a retail context	▪ Program adaption is stimulated by promotions and previous adopters. ▪ Adaption is negatively influenced by store distance.
Ashley et al. (2011)	Customer survey about relationship marketing programs	▪ Anticipated benefits, involvement with the firm, and shopping frequency have a positive effect on relationship program receptiveness. ▪ Inconvenience and privacy concerns affect intentions to join a program negatively.
Demoulin and Zidda (2009)	Customer survey in a grocery retailing context	▪ Perceived program advantages, previous behavioral and attitudinal loyalty, as well as the number of loyalty program memberships enhance the probability of adaption. ▪ Perceived program complexity and store distance diminish the adaption likelihood. ▪ The likelihood of adaption is independent of perceived risk (i.e. use of personal data).
De Wulf et al. (2003)	Conjoint analysis (context not specified)	▪ Consumer inputs (e.g., participation costs, purchase frequency, participation efforts, and personal data release) and consumer outcomes (e.g., program benefits and program duration) influence the likelihood of joining a loyalty program.
Gómez et al. (2012)	Customer survey in a grocery retailing context	▪ Search for variety, shopping enjoyment, inhibiting factors (i.e. effort and disadvantages of participation), and privacy concerns affect the participation likelihood negatively. ▪ Attitude toward loyalty programs enhances the enrollment probability.
Jang and Mattila (2005)	Partly open-ended questionnaire in a restaurant context	▪ Expecting promotion e-mails, difficulty in redeeming rewards, and carrying the program card are major concerns when deciding whether or not to participate. ▪ Expected benefits (e.g., savings) have a positive effect on the decision to join a loyalty program.
Kivetz and Simonson (2003)	Experiments in diverse contexts (gas station, department store, grocery store, credit card, and restaurant)	▪ Idiosyncratic fit (i.e. own effort relative to the effort of other customers) has a positive effect on the likelihood of joining a program. ▪ In case of high effort advantage, increasing requirements to obtain a reward (i.e. redemption threshold) improves the enrollment likelihood.
Kivetz and Simonson (2002)	Experiments in diverse contexts (car rental, retailing, and hotel)	▪ Increasing program effort (i.e. redemption threshold) reduces the likelihood of joining a program with necessity rewards, whereas the likelihood of joining a luxury rewards program remains unaffected from variations of requirements. ▪ Type of consumption effort (work-related versus pleasure-related consumption) has an impact on the choice between programs with luxury and necessity rewards, such that work-related consumption efforts lead to a higher preference for luxury rewards programs.

Table 4. (continued)

Author(s)	Study Description	Major Findings
Leenheer (2004), Leenheer et al. (2007)	Panel data analysis in grocery retailing	▪ Economic benefits (e.g., savings and discounts) and non-economic benefits (e.g., enjoyment of participation) have a positive effect on program membership. ▪ Privacy concerns diminish participation likelihood. ▪ Multiple cards possession (in other industries) improves adoption probability.
Liston-Heyes (2002)	Face-to-face interviews about travel behavior and frequent flyer programs	▪ Enrollment likelihood increases with household income, age, number of loyalty program memberships, program knowledge, purchase frequency, and number of household members.
Noble and Phillips (2004)	Focus groups, in-depth interviews, and semi-structured interviews	▪ Four categories of reasons why consumers refuse to join a loyalty program stand out: upkeep issues, time issues, benefit issues, personal loss themes.
Nunes and Drèze (2006)	Experiment with a liquor store loyalty program	▪ Enrollment likelihood increases with endowed progress (i.e. enrollment bonus when joining a program) and with the employment of a program medium (i.e. points) instead of accumulating pure purchases. ▪ The employment of a program medium intensifies the endowed progress effect.
Peterson (1995)	Qualitative consumer interviews	▪ Economic benefits (e.g., savings, discounts), special recognition, as well as ease and convenience of shopping are the main reasons for participation in a loyalty program.
Toh et al. (1991)	Hotel guest survey	▪ Low purchase frequency, reduced flexibility in choice, unattractive rewards, and registration efforts are the main reasons for refusing to join a loyalty program.
van Doorn et al. (2007)	Internet-based questionnaire about loyalty program memberships	▪ Privacy concerns have a negative impact on the number of loyalty program memberships. ▪ The number of memberships depends on personal characteristics (e.g., income, gender, age, relationship status).
Wendlandt and Schrader (2007)	Experimental personal interviews with bookstore customers	▪ Situational reactance has a negative impact on the willingness to participate in a loyalty program. ▪ Situational reactance is influenced by contractual bonds (e.g., fixed subscription periods or minimum purchases), economic bonds (e.g., switching barriers), and personal characteristics (e.g., importance of autonomous buying behavior and trait reactance).
Wright and Sparks (1999)	Interviewer-completed street survey in a retail context	▪ Gender is a key discriminator in loyalty program participation (women: 87% versus male: 55%). ▪ Economic benefits (e.g., rewards, discounts, deferred payment) and in-store promotion are drivers for program participation. ▪ Lack of store use, existing memberships, and inconvenience of registration are reasons for refusing a loyalty program membership.

2.2 Redemption Decisions

The second decision field, redemption decisions, refers to program members' decision whether or not to redeem a reward. In practice, a considerable proportion of accumulated program currencies remains unredeemed, with the consequence that many existing loyalty schemes exhibit surprisingly small redemption rates (e.g., Drèze and Hoch 1998; Lal and Bell; Lieber 2011; Smith and Sparks 2009). On the one hand, reluctant redemption behavior might be beneficial to ensure the cost-efficiency of a loyalty scheme (Drèze and Hoch 1998). Many companies report financial losses due to their reward programs, and they openly admit making their redemption policies more stringent to control these losses (Noble et al. 2014). On the other hand, however, redemption activities are of considerable importance in members' perceptions of the attractiveness of a loyalty program (Nunes and Drèze 2006b) and have positive consequences on future purchase behavior. As already stated, obtaining rewards has been shown to motivate participants to maintain and even increase purchase levels through a rewarded behavior effect (Smith and Sparks 2009; Taylor and Neslin 2003) and, thus, helps to attain program related objectives. Despite its significance, the investigation and explanation of redemption decisions received minimal attention by previous research (Noble et al. 2014; Smith and Sparks 2009). The limited literature addressing this decision field identifies two categories of factors influencing program members' redemption behavior; namely, program-specific parameters and customer characteristics.

First, program-specific factors include redemption thresholds, as well as value and attractiveness of rewards. More specifically, Drèze and Hoch (1998) evidenced decreasing redemption rates due to increasing redemption thresholds. This finding can be readily explained by the fact that high redemption thresholds entail a higher proportion of scheme members which exhibit insufficient cumulative purchase volumes to attain these thresholds. In addition, the authors proposed—though without empirical proof—that sheer forgetfulness might be an additional factor responsible for low redemption rates. In a similar vein, Smith and Sparks (2009) pointed out that saving loyalty points for high value rewards is a key reason for delayed redemption or—if the saving process is interrupted—non-redemption. However, according to Nunes and Drèze (2006a) endowed progress in terms of an enrollment bonus might help to prevent saving processes from being abandoned. Similar to its effect on participation decisions, reframing the point collection task as already begun, increases members' motivation to complete the saving process; resulting in higher redemption rates. Considering the value of rewards, results by Drèze and Nunes (2004) suggest that program members are more likely to redeem collected points for high value rewards rather than for small rewards. However, the likelihood to redeem points for low value rewards can be enhanced by employing a combined-currency pricing scheme. Moreover, perceived reward attractiveness was shown to positively affect redemption behavior (Liu and Brock 2009). Finally, it should be noted that redemption decisions do not depend on whether program benefits are economic or social (Noble et al. 2014).

Second, aside from program-related factors, customer characteristics contribute to an explanation of redemption behavior. Previous research has demonstrated that high purchase frequencies and spending levels are accompanied with more pronounced redemption activities (Lal and Bell 2003; Smith and Sparks 2009). Accordingly, the percentage of customers redeeming a reward is higher among heavy buyers than among moderate or light buyers (Liu 2007). Regarding the development of redemption patterns over membership duration, findings are inconclusive. Analyzing transaction data of a convenience store program, Liu (2007) found that redemption rates—especially of moderate and light buyers—increased over time. However, Leenheer (2004) as well as Liu and Brock (2009) have evidenced a significant negative relationship between membership duration and reward redemption for a clothing retailer program and a credit card program, respectively. Whether these contradicting results can be ascribed to different contexts of analysis remains unexplored. Table 5 summarizes previous empirical research on program members' redemption behavior.

Table 5. Summary of Research on Redemption Decisions

Author(s)	Study Description	Major Findings
Drèze and Hoch (1998)	Experiment with a beauty and health care products program	▪ Increasing redemption thresholds has a negative effect on redemption rates.
Drèze and Nunes (2004)	Experiments with frequent-flyer programs	▪ Individuals are more likely to redeem loyalty points for high value rewards rather than for low value rewards. ▪ People prefer combined-currency prices for low value rewards and single-currency prices for high value rewards.
Lal and Bell (2003)	Loyalty program data analysis in a grocery retailing context	▪ Redemption rate is highest among customers with high spending levels (i.e. heavy buyers).

Table 5. (continued)

Author(s)	Study Description	Major Findings
Leenheer (2004)	Transaction data analysis in clothing retailer context	▪ The face value of vouchers (based on past purchases) has a positive impact on redemption rates. ▪ Redemption rates also depend on previous redemption behavior. ▪ Membership duration has a negative impact on the likelihood to redeem a reward.
Liu (2007)	Transaction data analysis in a convenience store context	▪ Heavy buyers claim more of their rewards than moderate and light buyers. ▪ Redemption patterns change over time: in two years, moderate and light buyers' redemption rate increased stronger than heavy buyers' reward claim rate.
Liu and Brock (2009)	Focus groups and telephone survey about credit card loyalty programs	▪ Awareness about reward point program, average usage of credit cards, and attitude toward offered rewards positively affect redemption behavior. ▪ Negative relationship between duration of credit card usage and reward redemption.
Noble et al. (2014)	Experiment in a hotel context	▪ The likelihood of redeeming a reward is unaffected by the type of the offered rewards (i.e. social versus economic).
Nunes and Drèze (2006a)	Experiment with a car wash program	▪ Endowed progress has a positive effect on redemption rates.
Smith and Sparks (2009)	Transaction data analysis and qualitative thematic interviews in a retail context	▪ Number of visits, spending levels, and the number of purchased products have a positive effect on redemption rates. ▪ Saving loyalty points toward a particular redemption goal (e.g., high value rewards) is common and leads to delayed redemption. ▪ Saving processes for high value rewards are often interrupted by a variety of intercepting events, including goal switching and impulse redemption.

2.3 Purchase Decisions

Purchase decisions include, inter alia, consumer decisions regarding the types of products bought, their shopping frequency, and the monetary values spent on a company (De Cannière, De Pelsmacker, and Geuens 2009). Since the effectiveness of loyalty schemes is typically assessed by means of an examination of program members' changes in purchase behavior in favor of the target company's offering which are not evident among non-members (Dowling and Uncles 1997; Drèze and Hoch 1998; Sharp and Sharp 1997), it is not surprising that previous research paid special attention to an investigation of the influence of loyalty schemes on purchase decisions.

Extant literature on these effects can be classified into three categories. First, and most intuitively, to attain program-related objectives in terms of fostering loyalty, program schemes should increase customers' preference for the focal company. For this reason, previous findings on the effects of loyalty program memberships on brand and store choices are reviewed. Second, loyalty programs typically reward their members based on the dimensions of purchase volume, value, and frequency. Hence, the second section addresses loyalty program effects on these three facets of behavioral loyalty. Finally, as recent research has started to evaluate program effects on purchase patterns in terms of customer shares (e.g., share-of-wallet, share-of-purchase, and share-of-visits), findings on the impact of loyalty programs on these measures are summarized in a third step.

Considering the first category of research on purchase decisions, extant literature indicates that loyalty program memberships are indeed able to improve brand choice in favor of the target company (Roehm et al. 2002). In addition, previous research suggests that program members' brand preferences vary among different specifications of program design parameters. For instance, the likelihood of choosing the target brand has been shown to be positively related to the value of the offered rewards (Soman 1998), while being unaffected from their type in terms of tangibility and congruence with the company's products (Roehm et al. 2002). With regard to the issuance mechanism of reward points, van Osselaer et al. (2004) evidenced in an experimental study with fictive frequent flyer programs that different intertemporal allocations of the same quantity of loyalty points—i.e. ascending number of points (e.g., 100 points for each first, 200 for each second, 300 for each third purchase) versus descending number of points per purchase (e.g., 300 points for each first, 200 for each second, 100 for each third purchase)—affected individuals' airline choices. More specifically, although program efforts (3 paid tickets to earn a free ticket) and reward thresholds (600 points) were equal between programs, over each purchase decision, the likelihood of choosing an airline significantly increased with its competitive advantage in the number of credited loyalty points. Finally, findings on the role of required effort to obtain a reward in store and brand preference construction indicate a negative effect of increasing redemption thresholds on store and brand choices (Drèze and Nunes 2011; Soman 1998). However, as demonstrated by Drèze and Nunes (2011), this relationship is more complex. The authors evidenced that a decreasing attainability of rewards results in a higher likelihood of shopping at the target store as low redemption thresholds may fail to motivate program members. However, if redemption thresholds increase too much, this effect reverts as program benefits become unattainable which, in turn, demotivates participants. The following table 6 provides an overview of previous research on the effects of loyalty programs on customers' brand and store preferences.

Table 6. Summary of Research on Brand and Store Choice

Author(s)	Study Description	Major Findings
Drèze and Nunes (2011)	Experiment in a grocery retailing context	▪ The likelihood of shopping at the target store is an inverted u-function of divisibility (i.e. number and attainability of rewards); store preferences increase with a moderate decrease in divisibility, but decreases with strong reductions.
Roehm et al. (2002)	Experimental studies with a soft drink company's program	▪ Program participation enhances target brand choice. ▪ Brand choice remains unaffected from type of rewards (i.e. tangibility and relatedness to favorable brand associations).
Soman (1998)	Experiment in a clothing retailing context	▪ Delay and face value of rewards have a positive effect on the likelihood of choosing the target brand. ▪ Program effort affects brand choice negatively.
van Osselaer et al. (2004)	Experimental studies in an airline context	▪ Intertemporal allocation of the same quantity of loyalty points has an impact on airline choice, such that the likelihood of choosing an airline significantly increased with its competitive advantage in the number of offered loyalty points.

Focusing on the second group of purchase decisions, a broad body of literature has investigated how loyalty program memberships alter purchase behavior regarding purchase volume, value, and frequency. Generally, program participants exhibit higher levels of behavioral loyalty than non-members (Bolton et al. 2000; Lewis 2004; Meyer-Waarden 2008; Meyer-Waarden and Benavent 2006, 2009; Sharp and Sharp 1997; Smith et al. 2003; Verhoef, Franses, and Hoekstra 2001). However, the comparison of purchase patterns among members and non-members might be subject to an endogeneity problem; i.e. customers with higher expenditure levels are more likely to enroll in a loyalty program (e.g., Demoulin and Zidda 2009; Noble and Phillips 2004; Toh et al. 1991) and, thus, the differences between members and non-members may already exist before program effects occur (De Wulf et al. 2003; Leenheer et al. 2007; Liston-Heyes 2002; Wright and Sparks 1999). Therefore, ascribing these differences completely to the loyalty scheme under consideration might overestimate its effectiveness regarding changes in consumer behavior (Leenheer et al. 2007; Liu and Yang 2009). However, studies accounting for such a self-selection bias through an assessment of behavioral changes after enrollment relative to program members' previous behavior exhibit similar positive, though smaller, program effects (e.g., Liu 2007; Taylor and Neslin 2005).

In addition, the influence of loyalty schemes on purchase decisions has been shown to vary across customer segments. Light and moderate buyers as well as new customers feature the strongest behavioral changes regarding spending levels and purchase frequencies, whereas heavy buyers usually maintain their high expenditures (Lal and Bell 2003; Liu 2007). However, these membership effects are not stable over time. In this context, Meyer-Waarden and Benavent (2009) demonstrated that subsequent to an initial positive short-term effect on purchase indicators such as basket values and purchase frequency (see also Drèze and Hoch 1998), purchase patterns converge to pre-enrollment behavior. More specific research on behavioral changes over time has identified two types of underlying mechanisms: a short-term point pressure effect and a long-term rewarded behavior effect (Taylor and Neslin 2005). The point pressure effect refers to a temporary increase in spending behavior as a result of program members' engagement to obtain a reward. According to Kivetz et al.'s (2006) goal-gradient hypothesis, this point pressure effect increases with progress toward a reward. In this context, it has been shown that endowed loyalty points when joining a program influence customers' perceptions of progress toward a reward and, thus, induce purchase acceleration. For instance, Nunes and Drèze (2006a) demonstrated this effect by means of a field experiment with a car wash loyalty program. Patrons were offered a free wash after accumulating eight paid washes. Half of the customers were handed out a stamp card requiring eight stamps, whereas the other half were provided a card which required ten stamps with two stamps already affixed. For both of the two experimental groups, the number of days between visits decreased the closer consumers got toward attaining the reward. Interestingly, subjects given the cards endowed with two points took, on average, 2.9 days less between visits than those possessing the card without the enrollment bonus (see also Kivetz et al. 2006). In contrast to the point pressure effect, the rewarded behavior effect refers to a long-term purchase increase, which is observable through higher spending levels among rewarded customers when compared to non-rewarded customers and, thus, alleviates the backslide to pre-enrollment purchase patterns after reward attainment (Taylor and Neslin 2005; Lal and Bell 2003; Lewis 2004).

Besides direct effects on purchase decisions, a few studies have addressed the moderating role of a loyalty program membership within established causal relationships. In this regard, Evanschitzky and Wunderlich (2006) revealed that the link between conative loyalty (e.g., repurchase and cross-buying intentions) and action loyalty (e.g., purchase frequency and spending levels) is significantly stronger for program members than for non-members. Similarly, Lacey (2009) confirmed an intensifying effect of program membership on the link between relationship commitment (i.e. attitude or desire for a company) and purchase increases. Table 7 provides an overview of previous research on the effects of loyalty programs on purchase frequency and spending levels.

Table 7. Summary of Research on Purchase Frequency and Spending Levels

Author(s)	Study Description	Major Findings
Bolton et al. (2000)	Customer survey and usage behavior data of a credit card company	▪ Members of a loyalty program exhibit higher usage levels than non-members. ▪ Program members are less likely to cancel the credit card service.
Drèze and Hoch (1998)	Quasi-experimental study with a health and beauty care category program	▪ Category program significantly increased total sales in the target category, the number of transactions, store traffic, and the total amount of money spent on target category per shopping trip.
Evan-schitzky and Wunderlich (2006)	Personal interview survey in a DIY retailing context	▪ Loyalty program membership moderates the link between conative loyalty (i.e., behavioral intentions) and action loyalty (i.e., purchase frequency, monetary amount spent).
Kivetz et al. (2006)	Experimental studies in diverse contexts (café reward program, frequent diner program, rating web site)	▪ Purchase frequency increases with decreasing goal distance. ▪ Illusionary goal progress (i.e. increasing the total original distance to the reward, while increasing the perception of the distance already completed) strengthens this effect.
Lal and Bell (2003)	Loyalty program data analysis in a grocery retailing context	▪ Loyalty program membership has a positive effect on spending levels. ▪ Program effects are stronger for lower spending customers than for heavy buyers. ▪ Reward redemption has a positive effect on basket size and shopping frequency.
Lacey (2009)	Customer mail survey in a department store context	▪ Loyalty program membership has a positive moderating effect on the link between relationship commitment (i.e., enduring attitude or desire for a particular firm or brand) and increasing purchases.

Table 7. (continued)

Author(s)	Study Description	Major Findings
Lewis (2004)	Transaction data of an online retailer	▪ The implementation of loyalty programs has a positive effect on purchase incidence rate, number of orders per customer, and spending levels. ▪ Receiving a reward in a prior period positively affects transaction value in the current period.
Liu (2007)	Transaction data analysis in a grocery retailing context	▪ After enrollment, consumers with initially low or moderate patronage levels purchase more and become more loyal to the firm; heavy buyers remain their purchase behavior.
Liu and Yang (2009)	Market data and online survey in an airline context	▪ Loyalty program membership has a positive effect on the frequency of flying with the target airline. ▪ The market share of the target company strengthens the relationship between membership and purchase frequency.
Meyer-Waarden (2008)	Panel data analysis in a grocery retailing context	▪ Program members exhibit higher basket values, purchase frequencies, and shares-of-wallet than non-members. ▪ Program participants have lower interpurchase times and switching levels.
Meyer-Waarden and Benavent (2006)	Panel data analysis in a grocery retailing context	▪ Only 2 of 5 loyalty programs under consideration have a positive impact on purchase frequency. ▪ Programs have little effect on attracting new customers. ▪ Members of loyalty programs are more likely to buy at multiple stores which are participating in the loyalty program than non-members.
Meyer-Waarden and Benavent (2009)	Panel data analysis in a grocery retailing context	▪ Program membership has a slightly positive short-term effect on individual purchase behavior (i.e. basket value, purchase frequency, and share-of-wallet). ▪ Loyalty program effects vanish over time.
Nunes and Drèze (2006a)	Experimental study with a car wash loyalty program	▪ Endowed progress (i.e., starting balance when joining a program) has a positive effect of purchase frequency.
Sharp and Sharp (1997)	Panel data of a multi-partner program	▪ Loyalty program members shop slightly more often at program partner brands and stores than non-members.
Smith et al. (2003)	Diary study in a grocery retailing context	▪ Average spending per visit and average visit duration are smaller for non-members than for members. ▪ Loyalty program membership marginally increases the number of visits.
Taylor and Neslin (2005)	Customer mail survey and transaction data analysis in a grocery retailing context	▪ Rewarded customers exhibit an increase in sales, which is not observable for non-rewarded customers (rewarded behavior effect). ▪ Loyalty programs have a positive impact on sales (point pressure effect).
Verhoef et al. (2001)	Customer data of an insurance company	▪ Loyalty program members are more likely to retain their insurance contracts and to purchase new insurance products at the company.

Finally, several studies have addressed the effectiveness of loyalty programs in terms of changes in customer shares. These shares, which are also commonly applied by practitioners, describe the extent to which customers concentrate their total amount of visits or expenditures ("wallet") within a product category on a specific company (e.g., Kumar and Shah 2004; Mägi 2003; Meyer-Waarden 2007). Thus, these performance figures integrate choice behavior and transaction values during a specific period of time into a single measure (Meyer-Waarden 2007). Although both share-of-visits and share-of-wallet are highly correlated, they are not necessarily interchangeable. For instance, assuming that purchase expenditures vary between multiple shopping trips, a frequently visited store may only be used for small purchases, whereas consumers shop for a larger proportion at other, less often visited, stores. Hence, factors which influence where customers make the majority of their purchases regarding volume might not be equivalent to factors determining the store location they visit most frequently (Mägi 2003).

In accordance with the above findings, loyalty programs generally have a positive effect on customer share development (e.g., Leenheer et al. 2007; Mägi 2003; Verhoef 2003). Moreover, analyzing market-wide scanner panel data of competing grocery stores and loyalty programs, Meyer-Waarden (2007) revealed that loyalty schemes can diminish the negative relationship between store distance and share-of-wallet. However, the fact that customers are often participating in multiple loyalty programs at once jeopardizes these favorable effects. More specifically, the simultaneous possession of competitive loyalty cards has been shown to have a direct negative effect on share-of-wallet and share-of-purchase, respectively (Mägi 2003; Leenheer et al. 2007; see also Meyer-Waarden et al. 2007) as well as a negative moderating effect by cushioning the positive relationship between program membership and behavioral loyalty measures (Noordhoff et al. 2004). In addition, regarding scheme design characteristics, program rewards (De Wulf, Odekerken-Schröder, and Iacobucci 2001) and program attractiveness (Wirtz et al. 2007) have been demonstrated to drive customer shares. Furthermore, switching costs between programs have a positive effect on share-of-wallet; especially in case of low attitudinal loyalty toward the company (Wirtz et al. 2007). Table 8 summarizes previous empirical research on loyalty program effects on customer share developments.

Table 8. Summary of Research on Customer Shares

Author(s)	Study Description	Major Findings
De Wulf et al. (2001)	Personal interview survey in a grocery and clothing retailing context	▪ Loyalty program rewards have a positive effect on behavioral loyalty (i.e. share-of-wallet and share-of-visits). ▪ This effect is mediated by perceived relationship investment and relationship quality.
Leenheer et al. (2007)	Panel data analysis in a grocery retailing context	▪ Loyalty program membership, store distribution density, and price attractiveness increase share-of-wallet. ▪ Competitive memberships have a negative impact on share-of-wallet.
Mägi (2003)	Store-choice diary and questionnaire survey in grocery retailing	▪ Program participation has a positive impact on share-of-purchase of the target retailer. ▪ Simultaneous memberships in competing programs influence share-of-wallet negatively.
Meyer-Waarden (2007)	Panel data analysis in a grocery retailing context	▪ Loyalty program membership improves the focal stores' share-of-wallet. ▪ Store distance has a negative effect on share-of-wallet. ▪ Program membership diminishes the negative relationship between store distance and share-of-wallet; especially when store distance is low.
Noordhoff et al. (2004)	Customer survey in a grocery retailing context	▪ Loyalty programs have a positive impact on behavioral store loyalty (i.e. share-of-wallet and purchase frequency); as long as the number of alternative programs is limited.
Verhoef (2003)	Survey data and customer database analysis in a financial services context	▪ Loyalty program membership positively affects customer share development and customer retention.
Wirtz et al. (2007)	Experimental study with a credit card program	▪ Perceived switching costs between reward programs are highly effective in driving share-of-wallet at low rather than high levels of attitudinal loyalty; this effect is stronger for attractive loyalty programs. ▪ The attractiveness of a reward program has a positive impact on share-of-wallet regardless of switching costs.

In conclusion, the above considerations point out that loyalty programs are generally able to affect customers' purchase decisions in favor of the target company. These positive effects can be either the result of a direct influence of program participation but may also stem from a moderating impact on the relationship between diverse determinants of purchase behavior (e.g., conative loyalty, relationship commitment, or switching costs) and behavioral loyalty. However, the effectiveness of loyalty schemes depends on several additional factors. In sum, the reviewed studies reveal that personal characteristics (e.g., spending levels and store distance) and environmental factors (e.g., competing programs), as well as program design parameters (e.g., program attractiveness, program rewards, and redemption thresholds) determine the extent to which loyalty programs achieve their intended impact on purchase behavior.

2.4 Reward Decisions

Finally, the fourth decision field, reward decisions, refers to the program participants' choice between multiple reward options. Since different customers may appreciate identical rewards differently, loyalty schemes generally offer their members a variety of reward options to satisfy customers' heterogeneous preferences (Kumar and Shah 2004; O'Brien and Jones 1995). Although previous research exposes the importance of being rewarded on future purchase behavior (e.g., Taylor and Neslin 2005), relatively little is known about program members' reward decisions.

In a restaurant survey, Jang and Mattila (2005) found that loyalty program participants generally prefer monetary (e.g., discounts or cash back) over non-monetary (e.g., special services or products) and necessary (e.g., gas or grocery coupons) over luxury (e.g., coupons for wine or facial massage) rewards. However, further research highlights that the preference for different types of program benefits depends on the level of required effort to achieve these rewards. In this context, it has been shown that redemption patterns vary by perceptions of effort in such a way that high amounts of requisite effort enhance the likelihood of choosing 'guilt-free luxuries' over necessity items (Jang and Mattila 2005; see also Kivetz and Simonson 2002). This finding is consistent with Arkes et al.'s (1994) investigation of individuals' spending behavior of windfall gains; i.e. unexpected incomes. The authors revealed that windfall gains are more likely to be spent on hedonic, non-necessity items. An additional investigation of the choice between hedonic and utilitarian incentives demonstrated that this decision is also affected by the nature of redemption activities. Whereas planned redemptions typically aim for hedonic rewards, impulse redemptions tend to focus on lower-priced necessity items (Smith and Sparks 2009). Aside from the preference between necessity and luxury rewards, effort requirements have been documented to shift preferences between other types of incentives. For instance, Kivetz (2003) showed that effort and intrinsic motivation systematically affect trade-offs between the probability and the value of (uncertain) rewards. The preference for sure-small rewards over large-uncertain rewards is an inverse u-function of effort, such that low and high levels result in low preferences for sure-small rewards, whereas moderate requirements foster the preference for large-uncertain rewards. Moreover, intrinsically motivating (e.g., enjoyable) efforts extenuate the likelihood of choosing a sure-small reward and, additionally, diminish the positive impact of effort on the preference for sure-small rewards. Finally, considering the choice between brand-related (i.e. direct) rewards and program benefits with no linkage to the company's offering (i.e. indirect rewards), Kivetz (2005) found that, in general, customers have a strong preference for brand-congruent incentives. Again, this preference is additionally affected by effort requirements such that the preference for direct rewards increases with higher amounts of requisite effort.

In sum, previous research on reward decisions has predominantly concentrated on the program design factor of effort required for reward attainment (see table 9). Although extant literature on product choices reveals a wide range of factors affecting consumer choice behavior—e.g., context (Dhar and Wertenbroch 2000; Okada 2005), variety (Iyengar and Lepper 2000; Tversky and Shafir 1992a), or personal characteristics (Ailawadi, Neslin, and Gedenk 2001; Kassarjian 1971; Westfall 1962)—these findings have not been transferred to the reward decision context.

Table 9. Summary of Research on Reward Decisions

Author(s)	Study Description	Major Findings
Jang and Mattila (2005)	Partly open-ended questionnaire in a restaurant context	▪ Program members prefer monetary over non-monetary and necessary over luxury rewards. ▪ The preference for luxury rewards increases with higher effort requirements.
Kivetz (2003)	Experimental studies in diverse contexts (e.g., groceries, hotel, and magazines)	▪ The preference for sure-small rewards over large-uncertain rewards is an inverse u-function of required effort; the positive effect of effort is diminished in case of intrinsically motivating (enjoyable) efforts as compared to low intrinsic interest. ▪ Intrinsic motivation has a negative impact on the likelihood of choosing a sure-small reward.
Kivetz (2005)	Experimental studies in diverse contexts (e.g., grocery store, gas station, and airline program)	▪ Consumers have a strong preference for earning effort-congruent (i.e. direct) as opposed to effort-incongruent (i.e. indirect) rewards. ▪ This preference increases with increasing effort to obtain the reward.
Smith and Sparks (2009)	Qualitative interviews in a retail context	▪ Planned redemptions tend to focus on hedonic items, while impulse redemptions focus on utilitarian and lower-priced rewards. ▪ Planned as well as impulse redemptions tend to focus on self-gifting.

2.5 Synthesis

The presented review classifies the large body of extant literature on loyalty programs into four key decision fields within loyalty program memberships and compiles central empirical findings within each choice context. In summary, previous research employs diverse methodological approaches ranging from qualitative research methods to uncover customers' motives and barriers regarding participation and redemption decisions over experimental studies for an examination of the effects of program characteristics to customer surveys and longitudinal panel data analyses to shed light on manifold aspects of real-world loyalty programs. In addition, this literature review assembles various factors which have been found to be influential in the identified decision contexts. On closer examination, these factors can be assigned to three categories; namely, program design parameters, customer characteristics, and environmental factors (see figure 3).

Figure 3. Factors Affecting the Key Decision Fields in a Loyalty Program Membership

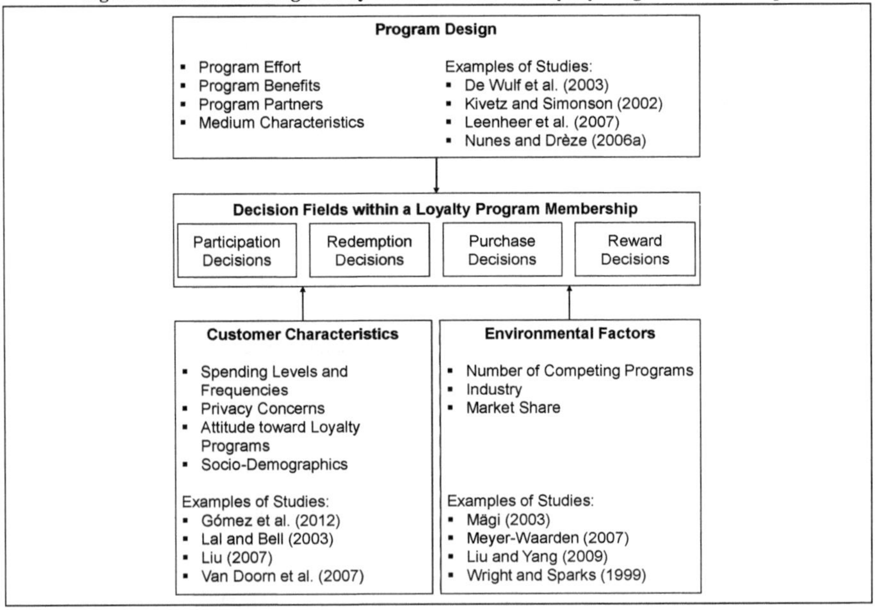

First, the investigation of program design parameters has been paid special attention by academic researchers. In this regard, program efforts (e.g., redemption thresholds, participation costs, and personal data release) and program benefits (e.g., types, value, and variety of rewards), as well as the number of partnering companies have been shown to be crucial factors for customer decisions. In addition, a few studies addressing medium issuance and redemption structures have evidenced that alleged irrelevant variations of specifications of medium characteristics (e.g., linear versus non-linear issuance mechanisms, enrollment bonuses, and single-currency versus combined-currency payment of rewards) influence consumer choices remarkably. Second, several studies reviewed highlight that not all customers respond to loyalty schemes in an equal manner. In particular, participation, redemption, and purchase decisions vary among customers characteristics (e.g., spending levels and frequencies, consumer attitudes, as well as socio-demographics). Contrasting the classical understanding of loyalty programs as an instrument mainly addressing heavy buyers (Liu and Yang 2009), extant research suggests that although frequent shoppers exhibit higher participation rates, moderate and light buyers are prone to stronger behavioral changes due to program memberships. Finally, the third category, environmental factors, clarifies that loyalty programs do not operate in an isolated setting. For instance, they often face competition from rival schemes. Indeed, simultaneous memberships in multiple programs have been found to affect participation and purchase decisions, such that loyalty schemes in markets with alternative competing programs have been shown to be less effective.

Overall, despite the abundance of existing loyalty program literature, understanding of the consequences of different specifications of medium issuance and redemption mechanisms is rather limited. However, a few studies corroborate the importance of research on program medium characteristics by highlighting their impact on consumers' perceptions of loyalty programs (Bagchi and Li 2011) as well as on purchase (Kivetz et al. 2006; Nunes and Drèze 2006a; van Osselaer et al. 2004) and redemption patterns (Drèze and Nunes 2004). Although these findings suggest that medium characteristics are not negligible program attributes and should not be determined by random, further research enhancing our knowledge regarding the effects of different specifications of medium characteristics lacks. In particular, given the fact that loyalty schemes in practice significantly differ in terms of the magnitude of their program currencies, it is surprising that the impact of medium magnitude on consumer choice behavior remains still unexplored.

3 Medium Magnitude Effects

This chapter outlines the basic idea of medium magnitude effects in loyalty programs; the central subject of this dissertation. Following this introduction, related phenomena—namely, medium maximization, money illusion and the face value effect, as well as numerosity effects—will be presented and discussed.

3.1 Definition

For the sake of argument, consider the following two supposedly equivalent frequently flyer programs, A and B, which solely differ regarding the magnitude of their program medium. Program A offers 1 loyalty point for each flight with the target airline and rewards its members with a free flight after accumulating 10 points. In contrast, the loyalty program B credits 100 loyalty points per flight and, consequently, requires 1,000 points for redemption. Whereas program A exemplifies a low medium magnitude, the program medium of scheme B exhibits a high magnitude (see also Bagchi and Li 2011).

Next, imagine a random passenger confronted with the decision whether or not to sign up for one of these programs. According to previous research on participation decisions, the decision to join a loyalty program is mainly influenced by the customers' assessment of the program outcome (e.g., a free flight) relative to its costs (e.g., the number of paid tickets required for redemption; De Wulf et al. 2003; Kivetz and Simonson 2003; Leenheer et al. 2007; Noble and Phillips 2004; O'Brien and Jones 1995; Soman 1998) such that the choice between participation and non-participation should be determined by the perceived value v of the outcome/input ratio of the loyalty program under consideration. Let $L_{join}(p; p, np)$ denote the likelihood of choosing participation p over non-participation np from the choice set {p, np} and, hence, the likelihood of joining the loyalty program. This likelihood can roughly be described as a function of the perceived value of the outcome/input ratio of participation. Thus,

$$L_{join}(p; p, np) = v\left(\frac{Outcome_p}{Input_p}\right). \quad (1)$$

This equation assumes that an increasing perceived value of the outcome/input ratio of program participation is associated with a higher likelihood of choosing participation over non-participation. Vice versa, if the loyalty program's outcome/effort ratio is low, dominance of the participation option over the non-participation option should vanish, resulting in a less likely enrollment. With regard to our passenger thinking about signing up for one of the above described loyalty schemes, it should apply that—since both programs require exactly the same effort (10 paid tickets) for the exactly same reward (1 free ticket)—the traveler's likelihood of joining program A should be equal to the likelihood of joining program B.

However, as mentioned, the outlined programs differ regarding the magnitude of their program medium. Note that, while the nominal number of credited points per flight depends on the specification of medium magnitude (1 point in the low magnitude program A and 100 points in the high magnitude program B) the value of these points in real terms (1/10 of a free ticket) remains unaffected from this attribute. Nonetheless, this nominal number may still be included as additional information into the enrollment decision. Let $v(m^{low})$ and $v(m^{high})$ denote the perceived value of the number of credited points in a low magnitude program and in a high magnitude program, respectively. This aspect is integrated in equations 2a and 2b which describe the likelihood of choosing participation p over non-participation np for a low and a high magnitude design:

$$L_{join}^{low}(p; p, np) = (1 - w) \cdot v\left(\frac{Outcome_p}{Input_p}\right) + w \cdot v\left(m^{low}\right) \tag{2a}$$

and

$$L_{join}^{high}(p; p, np) = (1 - w) \cdot v\left(\frac{Outcome_p}{Input_p}\right) + w \cdot v\left(m^{high}\right), \tag{2b}$$

where the relative weight w—ranging from zero to one—refers to the extent to which the nominal number in credited points is integrated into the participation decision. From a normative perspective, this nominal number should be of no relevance such that a rational decision maker should ignore this irrelevant program attribute and should focus the decision solely on the evaluation of the outcome/effort ratio of the loyalty program. In this case, the relative weight parameter w will take the value of zero with the result that both equations, 2a and 2b, become equivalent and, thus, medium magnitude has no effect on the participation decision. Consequently,

> *Medium magnitude effects are defined as differences in decisions within a loyalty program membership between consequentially equivalent loyalty programs which solely differ regarding the specification of their program medium's magnitude.*

For instance, medium magnitude effects appear if the likelihood of joining a low magnitude program and the likelihood of joining a high magnitude program diverge. Hence, if

$$L_{join}^{low}(p; p, np) \neq L_{join}^{high}(p; p, np). \quad (3)$$

Aside from the above described medium magnitude effect on participation decisions, redemption, purchase, and reward decisions might be subject to medium magnitude effects as well.

3.2 Related Phenomena

3.2.1 Medium Maximization

Individuals typically exert effort to obtain a desired outcome. However, in many situations the immediate reward they receive for their efforts is not the aspired return per se, but a medium (e.g., money as reward for work or loyalty points for repeat purchases) which still has to be exchanged for the desired outcome. Medium maximization refers to the phenomenon that, in situations involving a medium, individuals tend to focus on illusive immediate rewards rather than their final outcomes. Thus, when people are faced with choice options entailing different outcomes, the existence of a medium can alter which option they choose (e.g., Hsee et al. 2003, 2013; Hsee and Zhang 2004).

For instance, in one of Hsee et al.'s (2003) experiments, participants were asked to decide between a short task (6 minutes) which would award 60 points and a long task (7 minutes) which would award 100 points. Respondents were told that 60 points could be redeemed for a box of vanilla ice cream and 100 points could be redeemed for pistachio ice cream. In the control condition, in contrast, no points were offered, and the ice cream rewards for both tasks were simply presented. Although most respondents generally preferred vanilla to pistachio ice cream and, accordingly, most subjects in the control condition engaged in the short task, the majority of participants in the medium condition chose the long task. Hence, individuals exerted more effort to earn extra points although these additional points could not be used to redeem a more desirable reward.

From a normative perspective, individuals should ignore the medium and choose the option that leads to the highest outcome relative to its required effort. However, this experiment reveals that individuals tend to choose the option that is associated with the greatest medium return and, thus, fail to skip the medium; thereby overweighting the medium/effort ratio relative to the outcome/medium ratio. Aside from situations where a medium creates such an illusion of advantage, Hsee et al. (2003) described circumstances under which risky choices seem riskless and non-linear relationships between effort and outcome to be linear.

Consistent with the medium maximization effect, consumers are also apt to overweight the importance of the medium in loyalty programs. Accordingly, it has been shown that the employment of a program medium—i.e. accumulating points instead of purchases to obtain a reward—has a positive impact on the enrollment likelihood (Nunes and Drèze 2006a).

3.2.2 Money Illusion and the Face Value Effect

Today, customers are able to pay for diverse goods or services with loyalty points and frequent flyer miles such that loyalty program media have already acquired the status of a currency (Drèze and Nunes 2004; Liston-Heyes 2002). Hence, two phenomena which are present in the context of evaluations and judgments of currencies are also related to medium magnitude effects. First, money illusion reflects people's tendency to base evaluations of financial outcomes on nominal rather than real monetary values (Fehr and Tyran 2001; Fisher 1928; Shafir, Diamond, and Tversky 1997). Shafir et al. (1997) showed experimentally that individuals—when forming judgments about financial outcomes in times of inflation—rely on nominal face values and fail to assess the real (i.e. inflation-adjusted) value of money. For instance, a person who receives a 5 percent salary increase in times of 4 percent inflation is expected to be more satisfied than a person who receives a 2 percent salary increase in times of no inflation; even though the latter is better in real terms. These biased judgments toward nominal values might occur because nominal representations are relatively simpler and more salient than real values (Raghubir and Srivastava 2002; Robinson 1972).

Second, the face value effect documents biased evaluations of different currencies. This effect suggests that prices in higher denomination currencies are perceived to be more expensive than prices presented in lower denomination currencies (Lowe, Barnes, and Rugimbana 2012). For instance, analyzing individuals' spending behavior when using foreign currencies, Raghubir and Srivastava (2002) revealed that people tend to spend more in real terms when the face value of the foreign currency is a fraction of an equivalent unit of the home currency (e.g., US$1 = .4 Bahraini dinar). Conversely, when a unit of the domestic currency represents multiple units of the foreign currency (e.g., US$1 = 4 Malaysian ringgits) they are likely to spend less. In addition, the authors showed that respondents' willingness to pay increased with a decreasing face value of the currency under consideration. For example, respondents would pay 'only' 7377.45 Turkish lira (i.e. US$10.77) for a tie while they were willing to spend 150.58 Norwegian kroner (i.e. US$15.85). However, findings on the face value effect are mixed (e.g., Desmet 2002; Lowe et al. 2012; Wertenbroch, Soman, and Chattopadhyay 2007). For instance, when budgets and incomes also get transformed into the target currency, the opposite phenomenon—a reverse face-value effect—occurs such that consumers tend to overspend with an increasing face value of the foreign currency. Wertenbroch et al. (2007) argued that customers may take the difference between budgets and prices to form price judgments and assess how much money would be left after a purchase. Hence, if the foreign currency is more numerous, prices will appear less expensive. For instance, though economically equivalent, the remaining budget of 15.3 Singapore dollar (S$) for a product price of S$1.70 against a budget of S$17.00 seems higher than the remaining budget of US$9 for a price of US$1 against budget of US$10.

3.2.3 Numerosity Effects

Numerosity research, which focuses on the effects of alternative scales used to describe numerical information, constitutes a third related field of literature to which medium magnitude effects can be appended. Numerosity effects refer to the tendency to rely on the sheer number of units which serve to describe a stimulus—e.g., 1 (year) versus 365 (days)—as a cue for judging numerical information without paying particular attention to the unit used to express the information—e.g., years versus days (Pelham, Sumatra, and Myaskovsky 1994). An emerging body of literature (e.g., Burson, Larrick, and Lynch 2009; Gourville 1998; Pandelaere, Briers, and Lembregts 2011) evidences the presence of numerosity effects in a variety of different domains.

For instance, in one of several experiments Burson et al. (2009) confronted participants with the choice between two movie rental plans which differed regarding the number of included movies (7 versus 9 movies per week) and prices ($10 versus $12 per week); the authors found that respondents preferred the cheaper plan when the number of movies was presented on a per-week basis. However, although the amount of movies in each of the two plans remained unchanged, the more expensive option was preferred when the available movies were presented on a yearly basis (364 versus 468 movies per year). In a similar vein, Pandelaere et al. (2011) revealed that when choosing between two dishwashers with different warranty periods, a long warranty receives more weight when the scale used to provide the attribute information results in a large numerical difference between two warranties (e.g., 84 months versus 108 months) than when the description of the information leads to a smaller difference (e.g., 7 years versus 9 years). Similarly, individuals are more likely to donate $1 per day than $350 per year (Gourville 1998), the monetary value of many coins (e.g., 1 quarter, 2 dimes, and 17 nickels) is estimated higher than the value of few coins (e.g., 4 quarters, 2 dimes, and 2 nickels; Pelham et al. 1994), and a gamble with a chance of 9 out of 100 is preferred to a gamble with a chance of 1 out of 10 (Pacini and Epstein 1999).

C Theoretical Background and Hypotheses Development

The following part of this dissertation provides the relevant theoretical background and proposes several effects of a loyalty program's medium magnitude on consumer choices. Therefore, chapter 1 reviews theories of choice which provide the basis for the subsequent derivation of hypotheses regarding medium magnitude effects in each of the four decision fields in a loyalty program membership in chapter 2.

1 Theoretical Background

The relevant theories for an explanation of how medium magnitude influences consumer decisions can be classified into two categories. First, rational or normative models of consumer choice describe how a rational decision maker should decide between available choice options. In contrast, descriptive or behavioral theories are concerned with individuals' actual judgments and choices and, thus, explain why decision makers often derive from rational behavior (e.g., Baron 2009; Camerer and Loewenstein 2004; Simon 1959; Thaler 1980).

1.1 Theory of Rational Choice

Individual choice behavior is a widely studied research field and is of focal interest in diverse disciplines, such as economics, psychology, politics, and social science (e.g., Herrnstein 1990; March 1978; Simon 1959). The theory of rational choice provides a classical framework for a normative analysis of individual decision-making assuming that decision makers behave rational and aim to maximize their received utility (e.g., Arrow and Debreu 1954; Edwards 1954; Simon 1955). The following sections provide a general overview of this theory and its underlying principles.

1.1.1 Basic Model

This section outlines the basic idea of the theory of rational choice by the example of a discrete choice problem which refers to situations where individuals have to select one option among a finite number of different mutually exclusive alternatives (e.g., McFadden 1973, 1986; Ben-Akiva and Lerman 1985). Hence, continuous decisions, such as the quantity purchased, are excluded from the following considerations. However, such a choice situation constitutes a typical customer decision problem as it includes, for instance, the choice among different products, services, or brands. Formally, the available choice options an individual faces constitute a choice set C with J elements denoted by $x_i, \ldots, x_J$, i.e.

$$C = \{x_i, \ldots, x_J\}. \tag{4}$$

Next, individuals are assumed to be equipped with a utility function which assigns utility values to each alternative—i.e. $u(x_i), \ldots, u(x_J)$—which comprise all advantages and disadvantages and, thus, refer to the overall desirability of each choice option (McFadden 1986). Hence, the total utility of an alternative is a function—typically in the form of a linear combination (e.g., Debreu 1960; Einhorn 1970; Fishburn 1970; Luce and Tukey 1964)—of its attributes. For instance, a product (e.g., a laptop computer) can be understood as a bundle of more (e.g., processor speed and storage size) and less appealing (e.g., product price) product features (Erickson and Johansson 1985) which determine its total utility. This alignment of utility values allows that the available choice options can always be compared in terms of their desirability (Bettman, Luce, and Payne 1998; Fishburn 1970). Hence, considering a choice set $C = \{x_1, x_2\}$, comparison of the utility values of both choice options, x_1 and x_2, can either result in the finding that both options provide the same or different utility values, i.e.

$$u(x_1) \gtreqless u(x_2).^{2} \tag{5}$$

The basic assumption of rational choice theory is that individuals aim to maximize their utility and, thus, prefer the available choice alternative which provides the highest utility (e.g., Edwards 1954; Friedman and Savage 1948; Herrnstein 1990; McFadden 1986). In sum, it is implicitly assumed that the decision maker is completely informed about all alternatives and their consequences, infinitely sensitive to differences among choice options, and has the ability or skill in computation to make rational decisions that maximize the received value (e.g.,

[2] For choice problems under risk—i.e. situations where a particular choice is not only associated with one, single certain utility, but rather a set of different utilities whose realizations depend on future states—the above utility values are replaced by expected utility values (e.g., von Neumann and Morgenstern 1944; Friedman and Savage 1948) in the form of

$$EU_i = \textstyle\sum_{n=1}^{N} p_{in} \cdot u(x_{in}),$$

where $u(x_{in})$ is the associated utility value of choice option x_i in state n with an occurrence probability of p_{in}.

Bettman et al. 1998; Edwards 1954; Simon 1955; Slovic 1995). Thus, for two choices, x_1 and x_2, an individual must

(1) either prefer x_1 to x_2, i.e.

$$x_1 \succ x_2 \text{ if and only if } u(x_1) > u(x_2), \tag{6a}$$

(2) prefer x_2 to x_1, i.e.

$$x_1 \prec x_2 \text{ if and only if } u(x_1) < u(x_2), \tag{6b}$$

(3) or must be indifferent between them, i.e.

$$x_1 \sim x_2 \text{ if and only if } u(x_1) = u(x_2). \tag{6c}$$

Finally, choice models translate the above described preference and utility relations into choice probabilities which describe the likelihood of any choice option being chosen from a choice set as a function not only of the utility of the choice option under consideration, but also the utilities of all other available choice options. Let $P(x_1; x_1, x_2)$ denote the probability of choosing option x_1 from a choice set $\{x_1, x_2\}$ and $P(x_2; x_1, x_2)$ the choice probability of option x_2, it applies that

(1) $P(x_1; x_1, x_2) > P(x_2; x_1, x_2)$ if and only if $u(x_1) > u(x_2)$, i.e. $u(x_1) - u(x_2) > 0$, (7a)

(2) $P(x_1; x_1, x_2) < P(x_2; x_1, x_2)$ if and only if $u(x_1) < u(x_2)$, i.e. $u(x_1) - u(x_2) < 0$, (7b)

(3) $P(x_1; x_1, x_2) = P(x_2; x_1, x_2)$ if and only if $u(x_1) = u(x_2)$, i.e. $u(x_1) - u(x_2) = 0$. (7c)

Discrete choice models—e.g., maximum utility model, attraction model (Bradley and Terry 1952; Luce 1959), or logit choice model (McFadden 1973)—are generally similar with regard to the above described relations between utility differences and choice probabilities. However, they differ regarding the size of differences in choice probabilities between choice options which are associated with differences in utility values (see e.g., Ben-Akiva and Lerman 1985; Börsch-Supan 1987 for an overview of different choice models).

1.1.2 Principles of Rational Choice

The theory of rational choice implies the observation of several essential axioms—inter alia, the principles of transitivity, independence, and invariance are commonly considered as most essential (e.g., Tversky and Kahneman 1986; Read 2009; Li and Adams 1995)—which are outlined subsequently. Due to their concrete formulation, these principles have been subject to diverse empirically investigations examining systematic violations and, thus, deviations from rational decision-making as defined by the theory of rational choice (see e.g., Baron 2009 for a review).

1.1.2.1 Transitivity of Preferences

Probably the most basic principle of rational choice is transitivity of preferences (Tversky 1969). The assumption of transitivity implies that choices must be placed in order. Considering the choice among three alternatives—x_1, x_2, and x_3—a decision maker who prefers x_1 to x_2 and x_2 to x_3, must prefer x_1 to x_3 (e.g., May 1954; Tversky 1969; Tversky and Kahneman 1986). More formally, a preference or indifference relation ($\gtrsim$) is transitive if for all x_1, x_2, and x_3

$$x_1 \gtrsim x_2, \text{ and } x_2 \gtrsim x_3 \quad \text{imply} \quad x_1 \gtrsim x_3. \tag{8}$$

The essential role of the transitivity assumption for the theory of rational choice results from the fact that it constitutes a necessary condition for the representation of preferences by means of a utility function (e.g., May 1954; Navarick and Fantino 1974; Tversky 1969; Tversky and Kahneman 1986).

However, empirical evidence suggests that individuals may be prone to violations of the transitivity principle. For instance, preference cycles or preference reversals have been occurred in rankings of hypothetical marriage partners (May 1954), choices between applicants (Tversky 1969), and predominantly in decisions between lotteries and gambles (e.g., Lichtenstein and Slovic 1971, 1973; Loomes and Taylor 1992; Slovic and Lichtenstein 1968; Starmer 1999).

1.1.2.2 Independence Principle

The theory of rational choice further assumes that the preference between options does not depend on the presence or absence of other options (Luce 1959; McFadden 1973). More precisely, the independence principle states that the preference order between two choice options, x_1 and x_2, is independent of other available alternatives, such that if x_1 is preferred to x_2 in a binary choice, x_1 is also preferred to x_2 in multiple choice situations, as the presence of additional choice options does not provide new information about x_1 or x_2. In other words, a non-preferred option should not be preferred when new alternatives are added to the choice set (e.g., Tversky 1996; Tversky and Simonson 1993).

Again, previous research identified phenomena (e.g., asymmetric dominance, substitution, and compromise effects, as well as choice deferral and the omission bias) which are inconsistent with the independence principle. For instance, Huber, Payne, and Puto (1982) revealed a significant shift in choice shares when adding an asymmetrically dominated alternative—i.e. a choice option which is inferior to only one choice option but not to another—to a choice set for diverse product categories (e.g., cars, beers, and restaurants). In one of their experiments, participants were asked to choose among two six-packs of beers described by two attributes; namely, price and quality rating. Forty-three percent of participants preferred the target beer ($1.80; quality rating: 50) over the competitor beer ($2.60; quality rating: 70) which was, correspondingly, chosen by 57 percent of participants. However, adding a third asymmetrically dominated—i.e. 'decoy'—six-pack to the choice set ($1.80; quality rating: 40) which was dominated by the target but not by the competitor beer, increased the target beer's choice share to 63 percent. Hence, contrary to the principle of independence, although the presence of the asymmetrically dominated choice option neither provides new information about the target nor the competitor six-pack, respondents' preference order among these stimuli reversed. Table 10 provides an overview of selected additional biases which cause a violation of the independence principle.

Table 10. Violations of the Independence Principle

Bias	Definition	Examples of Studies
Asymmetric Dominance Effect (Attraction Effect)	Change in preferences between two options through the presence of a third option which is asymmetrically dominated, i.e. inferior to one option but not to the other.	Ariely and Wallsten (1995) Heath and Chatterjee (1995) Huber et al. (1982) Wedell (1991)
Substitution Effect	Adding an option to a choice set decreases the choice probabilities of similar options stronger than of dissimilar options.	Huber and Puto (1983)
Compromise Effect (Extremeness Aversion)	The addition of an option to a two-option choice set increases the probability of choosing the middle (i.e. compromise) option.	Simonson (1989) Simonson and Tversky (1992) Tversky and Simonson (1993)
Choice Deferral and Omission Bias	Adding an option to a choice set increases the probability of choosing a non-option (i.e. choice deferral or omission).	Iyengar and Lepper (2000) Redelmeier and Shafir (1995) Ritov and Baron (1990) Tversky and Shafir (1992a)

1.1.2.3 Invariance Principle

Finally, the last fundamental requirement of rational choice is the principle of invariance (Arrow 1982; Kahneman and Tversky 1979). This principle demands that preferences among different choice options are independent of their representation. Accordingly, different descriptions of the same problem which do not affect actual outcomes should result in the same choice (e.g., Bettman et al. 1998; Kahneman and Tversky 1984; Tversky 1996; Tversky and Kahneman 1986). However, extant research indicates that individuals deviate from rational decision-making such that the requirement of invariance cannot generally be fulfilled.

For instance, Tversky and Kahneman (1981) confronted subjects with a hypothetical choice between two alternative programs, A and B, meant to combat a disease which is expected to kill 600 people. Program A would save 200 people, whereas program B would save all 600 with a probability of .33 and no people with a probability of .67. Seventy-two percent of participants preferred program A to program B. However, reframing of the choice presentation—i.e. program A: 400 people will die; program B: .33 probability that no people will die and .67 probability that 600 people will die—led to a significant preference shift, such that only 22 percent of participants preferred option A to B. Although both choice problems were essentially equivalent, providing the information about both programs in terms of gains (lives saved) as opposed to losses (lives lost) causes a preference reversal. In addition to this framing effect, previous research has evidenced further cognitive biases which violate the invariance condition (see table 11). Note that, the existence of already described phenomena of medium maximization, as well as face value and numerosity effects[3] also constitute a violation of the principle of invariance. Moreover, since the magnitude of a loyalty program medium merely influences the nominal number of medium units which are credited for every purchase as well as the nominal prices of rewards but not their values in real terms—and, thus, neither affects the program outcome nor its requisite effort—the existence of medium magnitude effects in loyalty programs would also violate the invariance assumption.

Table 11. Violations of the Invariance Principle

Bias	Definition	Examples of Studies
Framing Effects for Gains and Losses (Loss Aversion)	Outcomes are perceived relative to a reference outcome such that variations of the reference point determine whether a given outcome is evaluated as a gain or as a loss. Framing outcomes either as gains or as losses can cause preference reversals.	Tversky and Kahneman (1981, 1986) Kahneman and Tversky (1979, 1984)
Prominence Effect	Preferences inferred from choice are more likely to be in favor of the alternative that is superior with regard to the most important attribute than are preferences inferred from matching (direct trade-off) judgments.	Carmon and Simonson (1998) Fischer et al. (1999) Fischer and Hawkins (1993) Tversky, Sattath, and Slovic (1988)
Status Quo Bias	Individuals have a strong tendency to maintain the status quo such that, ceteris paribus, designating a choice option as the status quo increases its choice probability.	Hartman, Doane, and Woo (1991) Ritov and Baron (1992) Samuelson and Zeckhauser (1988)

3 See part B, chapter 3.2.

1.2 Descriptive Theories of Choice

The above considerations point out that in many situations individuals act in a manner that is inconsistent with the theory of rational choice. Hence, though doubtless suitable as guides for intelligent decisions (March 1978), in these situations rational models might be problematic for predicting actual behavior. Therefore, the following sections introduce descriptive choice theories which are appropriate to describe derivations from rational behavior and provide the basis for the subsequent development of hypotheses regarding the effects of the magnitude of a loyalty program currency on consumer choices.

1.2.1 Prospect Theory

The prospect theory (Kahneman and Tversky 1979) contributes to an explanation of several of the above outlined violations of the principles of rational choice. However, similar to the theory of rational choice, this approach assumes that individuals, when choosing among available alternatives, seek to select the choice option which maximizes their received outcome. Nonetheless, several disparities stand out.

Prospect theory structures the choice process in two stages; namely, editing phase and evaluation phase. First, the editing phase involves an initial analysis of the choice problem and its reformulation in a simplified manner to facilitate subsequent evaluation and choice (Kahneman and Tversky 1979; Tversky and Kahneman 1981). For instance, this simplification includes coding of the outcomes of choice options as gains or losses relative to a neutral reference point, cancellation of irrelevant information, and rounding of outcomes. Thereafter, in the evaluation phase, the edited available options are evaluated by applying a value function which assigns subjective values to the outcome of each choice option and, thus, can be understood as counterpart of the utility function of rational choice theory. Finally, the alternative with the highest perceived value is selected.[4] Figure 4 illustrates an asymmetrically

[4] For choice problems under risk, the weighted value V_i of an option x_i with N different realizations is given by

$$V_i = \sum_{n=1}^{N} w(p_{in}) \cdot v(x_{in}),$$

where $v(x_{in})$ is the perceived value of the outcome x_i in state n according to the subsequently described value function, p_{in} is the perceived probability of the outcome x_i in state n, and $w(p_{in})$ is the probability-weighting function which transforms probabilities into decision weights. The probability-weighting function proposed by Kahneman and Tversky (1979) suggests that small probabilities are generally overweighted, whereas moderate and large probabilities are underweighted (Kahneman and Tversky 1979, 1986; Tversky and Kahneman 1981).

S-shaped value function as proposed by Kahneman and Tversky (1979) and points to its three key properties.

First, in accordance with Markowitz (1952), the value function is defined on positive and negative deviations, i.e. gains and losses, from a neutral reference point, which is assigned the value of zero. This property implies that outcomes are not perceived in absolute terms rather than as relative differences from a base state (e.g., Kahneman and Tversky 1979; Tversky and Kahneman 1981, 1986, 1991). This feature also captures that changes in the reference point and, thereby, framing equivalent outcomes either as gains or as losses, can alter decisions (Kahneman and Tversky 1979; Thaler 1985).

Figure 4. The Prospect Theory's Value Function[5]

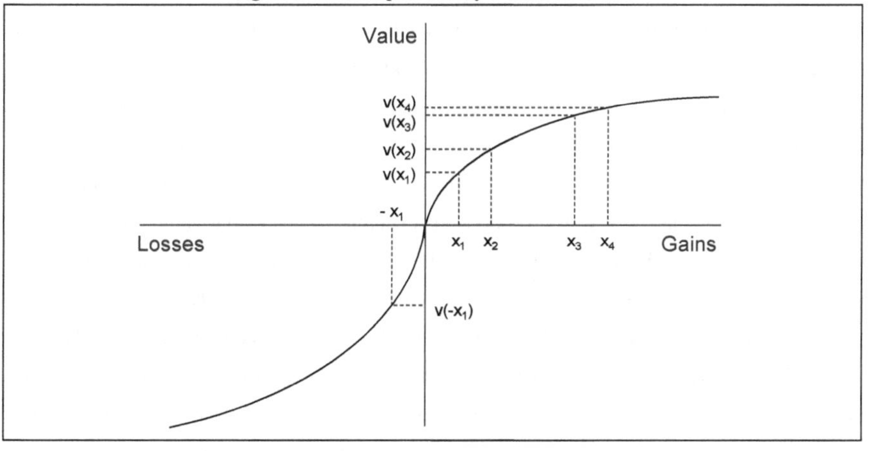

The second salient feature of the proposed function is that its assumed shape is concave for gains and convex for losses, such that the marginal value of both gains and losses decreases with their size (Tversky and Kahneman 1991). With regards to figure 4, this characteristic suggests that—though equivalent in absolute terms—the difference between x_1 and x_2 (e.g., \$10 and \$20) appears greater than the difference between x_3 and x_4 (e.g., \$110 and \$120; Thaler 1980, 1985), i.e.

$$|v(x_1) - v(x_2)| > |v(x_3) - v(x_4)|.^6 \qquad (9)$$

[5] Kahneman and Tversky (1979).

[6] The same applies to the loss area of the value function.

Accordingly, people are more likely to incur extra effort (e.g., a 20 minutes' drive) to save $5 on a calculator for $15 than on a jacket for $125 (Tversky and Kahneman 1981). In addition, this property also implies that individuals are risk aversive in the domain of gains and risk seeking in the domain of losses (Thaler 1980).

Third, the value function is steeper for losses than for gains, such that losses are perceived to be higher than gains in the same amount. By way of illustration, let x_i and $-x_i$ denote a gain and a corresponding loss relative to the neutral reference point, it applies that

$$|v(-x_i)| > v(x_i). \tag{10}$$

This asymmetry between positive and negative outcomes explains the phenomenon of loss aversion—i.e. individuals' tendency to prefer avoiding losses to obtaining gains (Kahneman, Knetsch, and Thaler 1991; Kahneman and Tversky 1984; Tversky and Kahneman 1991). Accordingly, it has been shown that people demand more money as compensation for giving up an object than they are willing to pay in order to acquire the same object (e.g., Carmon and Ariely 2000; Kahneman et al. 1990, 1991; Knetsch, Tang, and Thaler 2001; Thaler 1980; Tversky and Kahneman 1991). The property of different slopes of the value function in the domain of gains and in the loss area further implies that the marginal utility of additional gains decreases faster than the marginal disutility of increasing losses (Levy 1992).

In sum, prospect theory constitutes an important theoretical framework for the explanation of several deviations from rational behavior as defined by the theory of rational choice. Since this theory provides a basis for a better understanding of how choice problems are mentally processed and how decision makers evaluate available information, it might be an appropriate approach for a theoretical explanation of medium magnitude effects as well.

1.2.2 Anchoring and Adjustment Heuristic

The anchoring and adjustment heuristic (Tversky and Kahneman 1974) constitutes another source for an explanation of biased evaluations and decision-making. This heuristic refers to situations in which individuals make numerical judgments based on an initial value as a starting point, i.e. an anchor, which is subsequently adjusted until an acceptable final value has been reached. This adjustment is typically insufficient as final values tend to be close to the starting points, such that different anchors lead to different final judgments (e.g., Epley and Gilovich 2001, 2006; Tversky and Kahneman 1974).

For instance, in one of their studies Tversky and Kahneman (1974) asked participants to estimate the percentage of African countries who were members of the United Nations. By spinning a wheel in the subjects' presence, a random anchor between 0 and 100 was generated. Participants were first asked whether the percentage of African countries is higher or lower than the given anchor and, subsequently, to indicate their final estimate. The median estimate of participants with an anchor value of 10 was 25 percent, whereas participants whose anchor was 65 provided a median estimate of 45 percent. This finding demonstrates that even arbitrarily selected anchors affect numerical estimates to a considerable extent.

The biased evaluation process is characterized by two elements; the anchoring effect, i.e. the acceptance of random or informative values as starting points, and deficient adjustment. A widely adopted explanation for the anchoring effect argues that a temporary presentation of a numerical anchor is inadvertently saved in short-term memory. People subsequently, when asked about numerical estimates, consider any number in short-term memory independent of its source as a possible answer which results in biased numerical judgments toward the anchor (e.g., Chapman and Johnson 1994, 1999; Strack and Mussweiler 1997; Wilson et al. 1996). Considering the reasons for insufficient adjustment processes, Epley and colleagues (Epley and Gilovich 2006; Epley et al. 2004) have proposed that individuals stop adjusting once their reached estimate falls within an implicit range of plausible values. Therefore, estimates tend to lie near the anchor side of their range of feasible values. In addition, adjustment is effortful and, thus, is determined by the individual's attention and motivation.

The anchoring and adjustment heuristic has been found to be a good descriptor of people's evaluations in diverse contexts including distance (Raghubir and Krishna 1996; Wong and Kwong 2000) and volume estimations (Raghubir and Krishna 1999), purchase quantity decisions (Wansink, Kent, and Hoch 1998), monetary judgments (Howard and Kerin 2006;

Jonas et al. 2002; Mazumdar, Raj, and Sinha 2005; Raghubir and Srivastava 2002), as well as negotiations (e.g., Kristensen and Garling 1997; Liebert et al. 1968) and clinical judgments (Friedlander and Stockman 1983). In addition, violations of the invariance principle of rational choice (Slovic 1995) and the above described phenomena of face value and numerosity effects are often ascribed to biased anchoring and adjustment processes (e.g., Raghubir and Srivastava 2002; Pelham et al. 1994). Hence, this heuristic is additionally employed to explain medium magnitude effects in loyalty programs.

1.2.3 Reason-Based Choice

Individuals usually have the intention to provide good reasons for decisions they make to themselves and others (e.g., Shafir, Simonson, and Tversky 1993; Slovic 1975, 1990; Tversky and Shafir 1992b). Because such explanations are often needed, consumers are likely to anticipate having to give reasons during decision-making processes (Simonson 1989; Simonson and Nowlis 2000). This idea is adopted by the approach of reason-based choice (Shafir et al. 1993; Simonson 1989) which suggests that, especially in the absence of a clearly superior choice option, decision makers seek for reasons to justify choices for or against available options (Shafir et al. 1993). Through taking into account that relations among available choice options also affect choice by providing a convincing rationale for choosing certain alternatives over others, this approach sheds light on systematic violations of the independence principle of rational choice theory (Shafir et al. 1993; Simonson 1989). For instance, the already mentioned asymmetric dominance and compromise effects are two manifestations of reason-based choice.

Recall that the asymmetric dominance effect which describes the phenomenon that the addition of an option to a choice set which is dominated by only one alternative and not by another increases the choice probability of the dominating alternative (Huber et al. 1982). The compromise effect, in contrast, refers to the finding that adding an extreme option to a choice set increases the choice probability of the choice alternative which changes its relative position towards an intermediate option (Simonson 1989).

By way of illustration, consider the two options, A and B, mapped in figure 5. Suppose there are two attributes which describe these options such that B is better than A regarding the first attribute while A is better than B along the second attribute. In both cases, adding alternative C to the choice set increases the choice probability of option B.

Figure 5. Asymmetric Dominance and Compromise Effect[7]

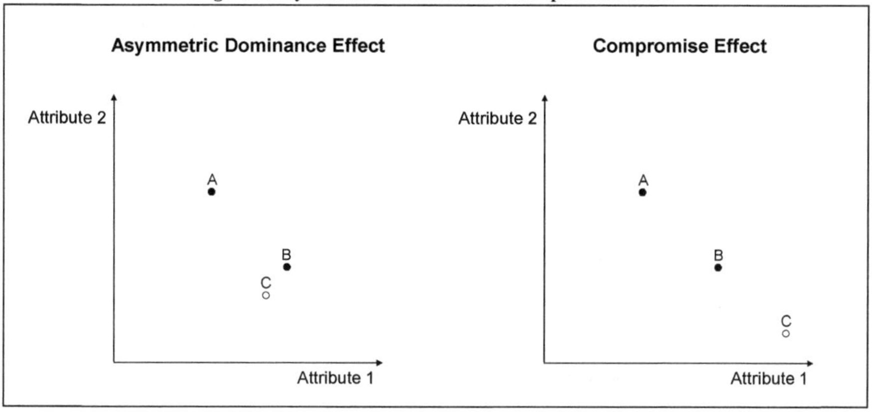

To make this clearer, consider the following experiment conducted by Simonson and Tversky (1992); similar to the above described study involving beer six-packs. One group of subjects was confronted with the choice between $6 in cash (option A) and an elegant Cross pen (option B). Thirty-six percent of the participants chose the pen, whereas the remaining 64 percent selected the cash. A second group of participants was offered a choice among the same two choice options, A and B, and a second, less attractive pen (option C) which was, consequently, dominated by option B, but not by option A. Only 2 percent chose the less attractive pen, but due to its presence the percentage of participants choosing the Cross pen increased from 36 to 46 percent.

The compromise effect can be illustrated by considering the following study (Simonson and Tversky 1992). Participants in one experimental condition were given a choice between two cameras: a Minolta X-370 priced at $170 (option A) and a Minolta 3000i priced at $240 (option B). Participants in the second condition were offered an additional option, the Minolta 7000i priced at $470 (option C). Both cameras in the first condition reached a choice share of 50 percent. However, option B (57%) was significantly preferred to option A (22%) when it became the middle option through the introduction of option C (21%). Hence, adding an extreme option to the choice set reduced the preference for the other extreme option, but not for the intermediate alternative.

7 E.g., Huber et al. (1982); Simonson (1989); Simonson and Tversky (1992).

Both the asymmetric dominance and the compromise effect are the result of people's intention to find compelling reasons for their choices. The fact that option B is better than option A along the first attribute (e.g., price), but A is better than B regarding the second attribute (e.g., quality or performance) produces a choice conflict if the decision maker contends with determining whether the advantage in attribute 1 compensates the disadvantage in attribute 2 and vice versa. However, in both cases the presence of alternative C offers a simple way to resolve this conflict by providing an argument for choosing option B; either through being superior to at least one choice option or through becoming a compromise alternative such that a decision in its favor is typically easier to justify than choosing an extreme option (e.g., Shafir et al. 1993; Simonson 1989).

In addition, whereas the above discussed examples reveal that relationships between competing alternatives may serve to find a conclusive rationale for and against available options which is easy to explain and to justify, other factors such as striking positive or negative features of a choice option (Shafir 1993) and even normatively irrelevant features (e.g., Brown and Carpenter 2000; Simonson, Carmon, and O'Curry 1994; Simonson, Nowlis, and Simonson 1993) can provide reasons for choices as well.

The effects arising from reason-based choice have been found for a variety of decision contexts including consumer decisions (e.g., Ariely and Wallsten 1995; Huber et al. 1982; Simonson 1989), gambles (e.g., Herne 1999; Simonson and Nowlis 2000; Tversky and Shafir 1992b), apartment (Tversky and Shafir 1992a) and workplace choices (Highhouse 1996; Slaughter, Sinar, and Highhouse 1999), as well as medical decisions (Connolly and Reb 2012; Redelmeier and Shafir 1995). In the present dissertation, this approach builds the basis for an explanation as to when and why the magnitude of a loyalty program medium might serve to justify customer decisions associated with program memberships.

2 Hypotheses Development

Drawing on the above described choice theories, in this chapter, the effects of medium magnitude on consumer decisions in a loyalty program membership will be derived. Due to an extensive similarity regarding the derivation of hypotheses, participation and redemption decisions will be considered jointly in a first step. Thereafter, these considerations will be extended and transferred to purchase and reward decisions. Finally, the empirical approach for testing the developed hypotheses will be outlined.

2.1 The Impact of Medium Magnitude on Participation and Redemption Decisions

When launching a loyalty program, motivating a significant number of customers to participate is a necessary first step in realizing the program related objectives. As a consequence, a better understanding of the effect of the alleged irrelevant specification of medium magnitude on participation decisions should be of great interest. However, mere participation is no guarantee for consumers to become more loyal toward the program provider. Thus, the finding that getting program participants to redeem their rewards entails favorable, loyal behaviors highlights the importance of redemption decisions on program effectiveness (e.g., Taylor and Neslin 2005).

Therefore, the following sections develop hypotheses regarding the effects of medium magnitude on participation and redemption decisions. In addition, with the intention of explaining as to when and why medium magnitude influences these decision fields, moderating effects are proposed.

2.1.1 Direct Effects

To understand how the magnitude of a loyalty program medium influences decisions in the participation and redemption context, one needs to consider how individuals perceive the nominal number of loyalty points that (a) are credited for purchases and that (b) are required to redeem a reward in a low and in a high magnitude program, respectively. Due to its assumed shape—i.e. concave for gains and convex for losses—the prospect theory's value function (Kahneman and Tversky 1979) provides a source for an explanation of medium magnitude effects in both contexts. A frequently replicated implication of this feature (e.g., Johnson, Herrmann, and Bauer 1999; Kaicker, Bearden, and Manning 1995; Lim 2006; Morewedge et al. 2007) is that segregation of multiple gains results in a higher perceived value than integration, whereas multiple losses loom larger in case of segregation than in case of integration (Thaler 1985). The following considerations explain this finding.

The value function was originally meant to assign values to single, unidimensional outcomes. However, according to Thaler (1985), this function might also provide conclusions about simultaneous multiple outcomes, such as, for instance, base rent and ancillary expenses of an apartment or base salaries and bonuses in the job context. By way of illustration, consider figure 6, which describes different possibilities of coding compound outcomes consisting of two equal components, i.e. x + x, and associated perceived values.

Figure 6. The Concepts of Segregation and Integration

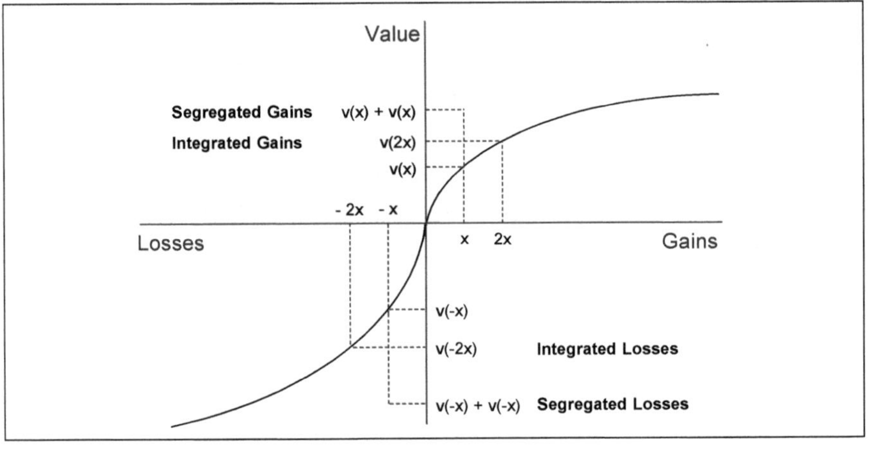

Generally, two types of the valuation of compound outcomes can be distinguished. They could either be integrated—i.e. valuated jointly as v(2x)—or segregated—i.e. valuated separately as v(x) + v(x). As can be seen in figure 6, the feature of the value function being concave for gains implies that

$$v(x) + v(x) > v(2x), \tag{11a}$$

such that segregation of multiple gains provides a higher perceived value than integration. For example, a person who wins twice in a lottery (e.g., \$50 + \$50) is estimated to be happier than a person who wins the same amount (e.g., \$100) in only one lottery. Vice versa, the feature of the value function being convex for losses implies that

$$v(-x) + v(-x) < v(-2x), \tag{11b}$$

such that integration is preferred. Hence, combining many small losses into one larger loss reduces the perceived total loss. For instance, a person who has segregated tax debts to different authorities (e.g., \$100 + \$100) is expected to be more upset than a person with integrated tax debts (e.g., \$200). These considerations allow the following two conclusions on medium magnitude effects on participation and redemption decisions.

2.1.1.1 The Choice between Participation and Non-Participation

By way of illustration, recall the above airline example where the low magnitude program A credits 1 point per flight and requires 10 points for a free ticket, whereas the high magnitude program B credits 100 points for every flight and, consequently, requires 1,000 points for a free trip. To derive the effect of medium magnitude on the choice between participation and non-participation, consider the following equation which roughly describes the likelihood of joining a loyalty program as a function of the outcome/input ratio of participation, the perceived value $v(m^{low/high})$ of the nominal number of credited points in a low and in a high magnitude program, respectively, and the relative weight w of incorporating medium magnitude into the participation decision:[8]

$$L_{join}^{low/high}(p; p, np) = (1 - w) \cdot v\left(\frac{Outcome_p}{Input_p}\right) + w \cdot v(m^{low/high}). \tag{12}$$

As the nominal number of points is only credited when choosing participation p over non-participation np, it can be interpreted as additional gain of joining a loyalty program. Transferring the principles of integration and segregation to the loyalty program context, it is assumed that this gain in a high magnitude program, m^{high}—i.e. 100 loyalty points in the above

[8] The derivation of this formula can be found in part B chapter 3.1.

example—is characterized by a relatively large number of points, each with a low value and, consequently, follows the idea of segregation, whereas m^{low}—i.e. 1 loyalty point in the above example—exhibits a small number of points, each with a high value, approaches the integration concept. As mentioned, the diminishing sensitivity of value function toward increasing gains implies that segregation of multiple gains results in a higher perceived value than integration—i.e. $v(m^{low}) < v(m^{high})$—with the consequence that the choice of participation over non-participation in a high magnitude program should become more likely. Hence,

$$L_{join}^{low}(p; p, np) < L_{join}^{high}(p; p, np). \quad (13)$$

In a similar vein, the anchoring and adjustment heuristic (Tversky and Kahneman 1974) which suggests that numerical judgments often are biased toward an anchor value offers an explanation for an increasing likelihood of joining a loyalty program with an increasing medium magnitude.

Considering customers' perceptions of loyalty programs, perhaps one of the most salient information is the nominal value of points credited for purchases. Therefore, individuals might be prone to use this nominal value as natural anchor to evaluate the attractiveness of participation. By means of the exchange rate between points and rewards this anchor can be adjusted to assess the true value of credited points in real terms and to form a final judgment about the loyalty program. However, it has been found that customers often misjudge the real monetary value of loyalty points (Liston-Heyes 2002) which indicates that adjustment in the loyalty program context might be insufficient as well. Similar to the finding that higher anchors lead to larger judgments (Tversky and Kahneman 1974), evaluations of high and low magnitude program currencies may also differ. Since the inaccurate adjustment process for a high magnitude program starts with a higher anchor, such a program is assumed to be perceived more attractive than a low magnitude program and, thus, should feature a higher participation likelihood. To conclude the above discussion, the following hypothesis is proposed:

H1a: *Medium magnitude has a positive impact on the likelihood of joining a loyalty program.*

2.1.1.2 The Choice between Redemption and Non-Redemption

Conversely, medium magnitude effects in the redemption decision context are expected to be negative. To adjust equation 12 to the choice between redemption and non-redemption, let $L_{\text{redeem}}^{\text{low/high}}(r; r, nr)$ denote the likelihood of choosing current redemption r over non-redemption nr—including future redemption—which is assumed to be a function of the outcome of a redemption activity (e.g., a free ticket) relative to its cost (e.g., 10 paid tickets) and the perceived value of the nominal number of points required to redeem the reward under consideration, $v(-m^{\text{low/high}})$—e.g., 10 points in the low magnitude design versus 1,000 points in the high magnitude program for a free flight. Thus, this likelihood can be described as

$$L_{\text{redeem}}^{\text{low/high}}(r; r, nr) = (1 - w) \cdot v\left(\frac{\text{Outcome}_r}{\text{Input}_r}\right) + w \cdot v(-m^{\text{low/high}}). \tag{14}$$

Since the nominal number of points required for redemption has to be abandoned and, therefore, constitutes a loss, and the feature that the prospect theory's value function is convex in the loss area—suggesting that segregated losses loom larger than integrated losses—imply that a high magnitude program currency—that follows the concept of segregation—increases the perceived costs of rewards and, consequently, should diminish the likelihood of redeeming accumulated points. Hence,

$$L_{\text{redeem}}^{\text{low}}(r; r, nr) > L_{\text{redeem}}^{\text{high}}(r; r, n). \tag{15}$$

In addition, it is expected that the nominal prices of rewards expressed in loyalty points serve as an anchor to assess the attractiveness of reward redemption. Because these nominal prices in a high magnitude setting are a multiple of the nominal prices in a low magnitude design, inadequate adjustment of this information leads to a more unfavorable perception of high magnitude prices. Hence, the following negative relationship between medium magnitude and the decision to redeem accumulated points is assumed:

H1b: *Medium magnitude has a negative impact on the likelihood of redeeming accumulated points.*

2.1.2 Moderating Effects

As mentioned earlier, from a normative perspective, variations of program medium characteristics neither affecting the program's outcome nor its requisite effort should be of no relevance to choice. Thus, the evaluation and subsequent decision to join a loyalty program should be merely based on its outcome/effort ratio and should not be influenced by the irrelevant magnitude of a loyalty program currency. However, empirical evidence confirms that irrelevant attributes can also influence consumer choice behavior (e.g., Brown and Carpenter 2000; Carpenter, Glazer, and Nakamoto 1994; Hsee 1995; van Osselaer et al. 2004).

According to the concept of reason-based choice (Shafir et al. 1993; Simonson 1989) people have the intention to have good reasons for the choices they make. Hence, individuals may initially seek dominance structures in decision problems because they provide the most compelling rationale for decisions (Montgomery 1983). However, when faced with equally attractive options that do not provide a clear preference order decision makers attempt to reach a reasonable choice by including irrelevant attributes as well (Shafir et al. 1993; Simonson 1989). Accordingly, it is expected that the relative weight w of integrating the irrelevant specification of medium magnitude into participation decisions depends on the dominance between the available choice options (i.e. participation versus non-participation). More specifically, in case of a low outcome/input ratio of the loyalty program a pure evaluation of the dominance criterion might not provide sufficient reasons for the choice between participation and non-participation. Hence, individuals are constrained to seek further information and, thus, are expected to include the perceived value of the number of credited points into decision-making. Conversely, if participation clearly dominates non-participation due to an attractive outcome/effort ratio, individuals will stop the decision-making process without elaboration of irrelevant attributes. Thus, the following hypothesis is proposed:

H2a: *The dominance between choice options moderates the relationship between medium magnitude and the likelihood of joining the loyalty program. A decreasing dominance strengthens medium magnitude effects.*

Moreover, hypothesis 2a should also hold in the redemption stage of a loyalty program membership. It is expected that, in situations where the dominance criterion does not provide sufficient reasons for the choice between redemption and non-redemption, people tend to incorporate the irrelevant attribute of medium magnitude to make a more reasonable choice. Hence,

H2b: *The dominance between choice options moderates the relationship between medium magnitude and the likelihood of redeeming accumulated points. A decreasing dominance strengthens medium magnitude effects.*

2.1.3 Summary

The above considerations focus on a theoretical explanation of medium magnitude effects on participation and redemption decisions. The developed hypotheses account for both direct and moderating effects. Based on prospect theory as well as the anchoring and adjustment heuristic it is expected that the magnitude of a loyalty program medium has a positive impact on the likelihood of joining a loyalty scheme, while it affects the likelihood of redeeming accumulated points negatively (see figure 7).

Figure 7. Hypothesized Effects of Medium Magnitude on Participation and Redemption Decisions

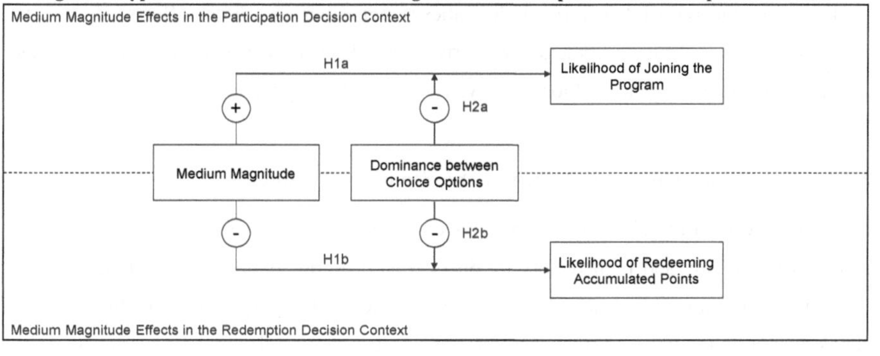

In addition, building on the concept of reason-based choice, it is hypothesized that the extent to which the irrelevant specification of medium magnitude affects decision-making depends on

the dominance structure between the available choice options in the participation and redemption decision context. Specifically, dominance between participation and non-participation as well as between redemption and non-redemption is assumed to moderate the effects of medium magnitude.

2.2 The Impact of Medium Magnitude on Purchase and Reward Decisions

By rewarding loyal purchase patterns, loyalty programs aim to influence purchase behavior in favor of the program provider. Such loyal behaviors are typically reflected in frequency, volume, basket sizes, as well as brand and store choice. To investigate the effect of the magnitude of a program medium on purchase behavior, the following section focusses on its impact on the choice between products of different quality (i.e. the choice between premium and standard products) which is directly related to sales volume figures. Analogously, in a next step, the effect of medium magnitude on the choice between premium and standard rewards is derived. Finally, potential boundary conditions are proposed.

2.2.1 Direct Effects

The following considerations broaden the above conclusions about the impact of medium magnitude on participation and redemption decisions to purchase and reward choices. Building on the same theoretical background, hypotheses regarding the direct effects of medium magnitude in both decision contexts are derived based on the concepts of segregation and integration of multiple gains and losses as well as the anchoring and adjustment heuristic.

2.2.1.1 The Choice between Premium and Standard Products

In accordance with the above considerations on participation and redemption decisions, the choice between low and high quality products should be predominantly determined by the outcome/input ratios of the available choice options. Let L(pp; pp, sp) denote the likelihood of choosing a premium product pp over a standard product sp from the choice set {pp, sp}. This likelihood can roughly be described as a function of the perceived value v of the difference between the outcome/input ratios of the premium product and the standard product under consideration (Birnbaum 1990; Fantino and Goldshmidt 2000; Rose and Birnbaum 1975; Wertenbroch et al. 2007), thus,

$$L_{buy}(pp; pp, sp) = v\left(\frac{Outcome_{pp}}{Input_{pp}} - \frac{Outcome_{sp}}{Input_{sp}}\right). \tag{16}$$

This equation assumes that the more the outcome/input ratio of the premium product exceeds the outcome/input ratio of the standard product, the higher the likelihood of choosing the premium product over the standard product. By way of illustration, consider the above mentioned airline example. Assuming that an airline offers an economy class flight for $100 and a business class flight for $200, the preference for the business flight should depend on whether its higher price (input) is justified by a commensurate added value (outcome).

In addition, similar to participation and redemption decisions, besides focusing on the outcome/input ratios, loyalty program members may also examine the nominal difference in credited points between the premium and the standard product when comparing the attractiveness of both choice alternatives. Since the monetary amount spent on the company most commonly provides the basis for point issuance (e.g., Bagchi and Lee 2011; Gómez et al. 2012; Liu 2007), the number of earned points in case of buying a higher priced premium product typically exceeds the number of earned points when buying a standard product. For instance, imagine that the low magnitude program credits 1 point for the economy flight and two 2 points for the twice as high priced business flight, whereas the high magnitude program credits 100 points for the standard and 200 points for the premium flight, respectively. Adding the perceived value of the nominal differences in the number of credited points when buying a premium product instead of a standard product—i.e. $v\left(m_{pp}^{low/high} - m_{sp}^{low/high}\right)$, whose relative weight for the purchase decision is indicated by the parameter w—to equation 16 leads to the following function:

$$L_{buy}^{low/high}(pp; pp, sp) = (1 - w) \cdot v\left(\frac{Outcome_{pp}}{Input_{pp}} - \frac{Outcome_{sp}}{Input_{sp}}\right) + w \cdot v\left(m_{pp}^{low/high} - m_{sp}^{low/high}\right). \tag{17}$$

Note that, while the nominal difference in credited points for buying the premium product instead of the standard product depends on the specification of medium magnitude the difference in real terms remains still unaffected. Nonetheless, two theoretical explanations offer themselves for why the magnitude of these nominal differences may influence purchase decisions.

First, as these differences can be interpreted as additional gain of buying a premium product instead of a standard product, the principles of integration and segregation allow a prediction of diverging perceptions of these nominal differences between a low and a high magnitude program. It is assumed that this gain in a high magnitude program—i.e. $\left(m_{pp}^{high} - m_{sp}^{high}\right)$ = 200 points – 100 points = 100 points in the airline example—which is characterized by a relatively large number of points, each with a low value, approaches the segregation idea, whereas the difference $\left(m_{pp}^{low} - m_{sp}^{low}\right)$—i.e. 2 points – 1 point = 1 point in the above example—which exhibits a small number of points, each with a high value, represents the integration concept. As already stated, segregated gains are associated with higher perceived values than integrated gains, such that the likelihood of choosing the premium product should increase with medium magnitude. Hence,

$$L_{buy}^{low}(pp; pp, sp) < L_{buy}^{high}(pp; pp, sp). \qquad (18)$$

Second, according to the anchoring and adjustment heuristic (Tversky and Kahneman 1974), people's evaluation of the attractiveness of choosing a premium product instead of a standard product might be biased if they rely on the nominal difference in the number of credited points as a cue for their judgment. Specifically, individuals are expected to use this difference as an anchor which is, subsequently, insufficiently adjusted. Since inadequate adjustment processes tend to stop near the original starting point, estimations of the real value of the nominal differences in credited points should be higher in a high magnitude program than in a low magnitude program. Consequently, the following hypothesis should hold:

H3a: *Medium magnitude has a positive effect on the likelihood of buying a premium product over a standard product.*

2.2.1.2 The Choice between Premium and Standard Rewards

In contrast, the effect of medium magnitude on the likelihood of choosing a premium reward pr over a standard reward sr—i.e. $L_{redeem}^{low/high}(pr; pr, sr)$—should be negative. Adjustment of equation 17 to the reward decision context leads to:

$$L_{redeem}^{low/high}(pr; pr, sr) = (1 - w) \cdot v\left(\frac{Outcome_{pr}}{Input_{pr}} - \frac{Outcome_{sr}}{Input_{sr}}\right) + w \cdot v\left(-\left|m_{pr}^{low/high} - m_{sr}^{low/high}\right|\right). \quad (19)$$

Hence, the likelihood of choosing a premium reward over a standard reward is expected to depend on the perceived differences in the outcome/input ratios of the premium and standard reward—i.e. the ratio between the respective reward and the number of accumulated purchases required for redemption—and the perceived value of the nominal differences in requisite points to redeem a premium instead of a standard reward. For instance, suppose that the exemplary low magnitude program A offers its members the choice between an economy flight reward for 10 points and a business flight reward for 20 points, whereas the same rewards are priced at 1,000 points and 2,000 points, respectively, in the high magnitude program B. Accordingly, when compared to the standard flight reward, choosing the premium reward in the low magnitude program entails additional costs of 10 loyalty points—each with a high value—whereas redeeming the premium flight reward in the high magnitude program requires an extra of 1,000 points—each with a commensurate low value. Thus, this nominal price premium constitutes an additional loss of redeeming the premium reward and—as integration of losses should be preferred—is perceived to be higher in a high magnitude program than in a low magnitude design. Consequently,

$$L_{redeem}^{low}(pr; pr, sr) > L_{redeem}^{high}(pr; pr, sr). \quad (20)$$

In addition, the anchoring and adjustment heuristic (Tversky and Kahneman 1974) implies that estimations of the real additional costs of redeeming a premium reward instead of a standard reward might vary with their nominal price differences expressed in loyalty points. Hence, since this nominal difference in the low magnitude program is smaller than in the high magnitude program, inaccurate adjustment entails that the price premium of premium rewards will appear to be less expensive. These considerations lead to the following hypothesis:

H3b: *Medium magnitude has a negative effect on the likelihood of redeeming a premium reward over a standard reward.*

2.2.2 Moderating Effects

Again, the reason-based choice conception which suggests that consumer preferences are based on various reasons which are constructed to justify decisions (Shafir et al. 1993; Simonson 1989) provides a source to identify a boundary condition of the impact of the normatively irrelevant specification of medium magnitude on purchase and reward decisions.

According to Montgomery (1983), decision makers initially focus on dominance structures between choice options as they provide the most compelling rationale for choices. Hence, people should focus on the differences in the outcome/input ratios between premium and standard products in the purchase decision context as well as between premium and standard rewards in the reward decision context. If these differences provide a clear dominance structure, individuals are expected to stop the decision-making process without paying attention to the irrelevant specification of medium magnitude. However, if the dominance criterion does not provide sufficient reasons for the choice between premium and standard product as well as between premium and standard rewards, people deliberately seek further information to find good reasons for their choice. In this case, individuals are prone to incorporate the irrelevant nominal differences (a) in the number of credited points when buying a premium product instead of a standard product as well as (b) in the number of requisite points to redeem a premium reward instead of a standard reward to make a more reasonable decision. The following hypotheses summarize this discussion:

H4a: *The dominance between choice options moderates the relationship between medium magnitude and the likelihood of buying a premium product over a standard product. A decreasing dominance strengthens medium magnitude effects.*

H4b: *The dominance between choice options moderates the relationship between medium magnitude and the likelihood of redeeming a premium reward over a standard reward. A decreasing dominance strengthens medium magnitude effects.*

2.2.3 Summary

The above discussion provides a theoretical derivation of the impact of medium magnitude on purchase and reward decisions. Drawing on the prospect theory and the concepts of segregation and integration of multiple gains and losses as well as insufficient anchoring and adjustment processes it is proposed that medium magnitude has a positive effect on the likelihood of buying a premium product over a standard product. However, with regard to reward choices, medium magnitude is expected to act in the opposite direction, such that the likelihood of redeeming a premium over a standard reward is negatively related to the magnitude of a program currency. Analogously to participation and redemption decisions, the concept of reason-based choice provides the basis to identify potential boundary conditions of medium magnitude effects. Hence, it is expected that if dominance structures between choice options—i.e. between premium and standard products as well as between premium and standard rewards—provide sufficient reasons for choice, the effects of medium magnitude will attenuate. Figure 8 provides a final overview of the proposed effects of medium magnitude on purchase and redemption decisions.

Figure 8. Hypothesized Effects of Medium Magnitude on Purchase and Reward Decisions

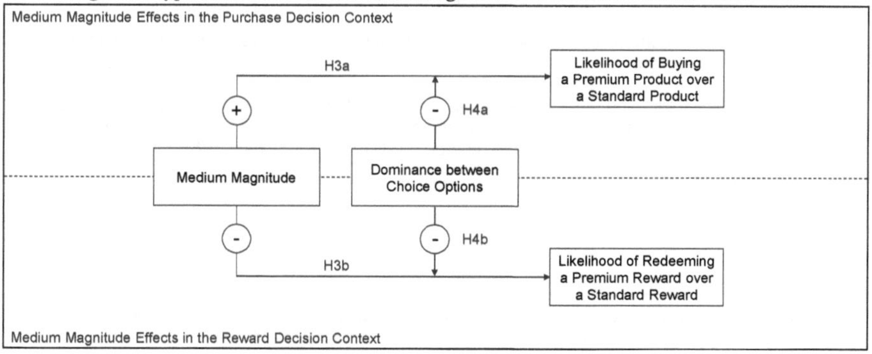

2.3 Empirical Approach

To empirically test the hypotheses presented above regarding the impact of medium magnitude on the four key decision fields in a loyalty program membership, each decision context has been investigated individually by means of three studies. Thereby, analysis of the proposed effects in each choice context follows the same procedure. For an initial test of the influence of the magnitude of a program currency, the first study in each decision field involves a simple choice problem such as, for instance, the choice between joining a low or a high magnitude program (study 1) or the choice between different rewards (study 9). The subsequent second investigation of each study series aims to provide further support for the identified effects and, additionally, tests the hypothesized moderating influence of dominance structures between choice options. Finally, the purpose of each respective third study is to confirm the external validity of the obtained findings by employing a heterogeneous sample structure. Table 12 provides a summarizing overview of the empirical studies conducted to test the theoretically derived framework on medium magnitude effects on customer choice behavior. They are documented in detail in the following part D.

Table 12. Overview of Studies[9]

Decision Field and Study	Study Context	Study Description (Dependent Variable and Hypotheses)	Sample Structure	Methods of Analysis
Participation Decisions				
Study 1	Airline programs	Choice between joining a low or a high magnitude program (H1a)	Student sample (N = 216)	χ^2-test
Study 2	Railway company program	Likelihood of joining the program (H1a and H2a)	Student sample (N = 123)	Analysis of covariance
Study 3	Stairs climbing bonus campaign	Choice between participation and non-participation in a bonus campaign (H1a)	Heterogeneous sample (N = 106)	χ^2-test, Fisher's exact test

9 Studies 2, 5, and 6 were presented at the American Marketing Association Summer Educators' Conference 2012 (Köcher and Blut 2012); Studies 7 and 10 were presented at the 42nd European Marketing Academy Annual Conference and at the American Marketing Association Summer Educators' Conference 2013 (Köcher and Blut 2013a, 2013b).

Table 12. (continued)

Decision Field and Study	Study Context	Study Description (Dependent Variable and Hypotheses)	Sample Structure	Methods of Analysis
Redemption Decisions				
Study 4	Airline programs	Choice between redeeming points in a low or in a high magnitude program (H1b)	Student sample (N = 187)	χ^2-test
Study 5	Railway company program	Likelihood of redeeming accumulated points (H1b and H2b)	Student sample (N = 124)	Analysis of covariance
Study 6	Real-world programs	Likelihood of redeeming a reward within the next 3 months (H1b and H2b)	Heterogeneous sample (N = 447)	Regression analysis
Purchase Decisions				
Study 7	Railway company program	Choice between buying a standard or a premium ticket (H3a)	Student sample (N = 79)	χ^2-test
Study 8	Supermarket program	Likelihood of choosing a premium shopping basket (branded products) over a standard basket consisting of private labels (H3a and H4a)	Student sample (N = 179)	Analysis of covariance
Study 9	Supermarket program	(Replication of study 8)	Heterogeneous sample (N = 227)	Analysis of covariance
Reward Decisions				
Study 10	Railway company program	Choice between redeeming a standard or a premium ticket (H3b)	Student sample (N = 87)	χ^2-test
Study 11	Railway company program	Likelihood of redeeming a premium ticket over a standard ticket (H3b and H4b)	Student sample (N = 196)	Analysis of covariance
Study 12	Real-world programs	Monetary value of redeemed rewards (H3b)	Heterogeneous sample (N = 292)	Regression analysis

D Empirical Examination of Medium Magnitude Effects

The following empirical studies systematically examine the effects of medium magnitude on the four key decision fields in loyalty program memberships. Specifically, chapters 1 and 2 address consumers' participation and redemption decisions, respectively. Thereafter, chapters 3 and 4 focus on loyalty program members' product choices in the purchase and reward decision context.

1 The Impact of Medium Magnitude on Participation Decisions

This section concerns situations where people choose whether or not to participate in a loyalty program. More specifically, the following studies aim to empirically validate the proposed positive effect of the magnitude of a loyalty program medium on the likelihood of joining the program (H1a) and to provide evidence for the moderating effect of dominance between choice options in the participation decision context (H2a) by systematically analyzing the elements of the already introduced function which roughly describes the likelihood of joining a program:

$$L_{join}^{low/high}(p; p, np) = (1 - w) \cdot v\left(\frac{Outcome_p}{Input_p}\right) + w \cdot v\left(m^{low/high}\right). \qquad (12)$$

The empirical test of the hypotheses follows a three-step approach. Study 1 is intended to offer initial insights into individuals' preferences for programs with mediums of different magnitudes through analyzing responses on a simple choice problem; namely, the choice between a low and a high magnitude program. Thus, this study concentrates on differences in the perceived value of the number of earned points between a low magnitude program—i.e. $v(m^{low})$—and a high magnitude program—i.e. $v(m^{high})$. However, the decision customers are typically confronted with is not which of several loyalty programs to join but whether to participate in a particular program that exhibits a specific level of medium magnitude. These situations are addressed in the following study 2. Besides the hypothesized effect of medium magnitude, this experiment tests the proposed impact of dominance between choice options which is expected to influence the relative weight w of incorporating the specification of medium magnitude into participation decisions and, thus, to moderate the medium magnitude effect. To provide a strong test of the proposed hypotheses, it is advised to use maximally homogenous samples (Calder, Phillips, Tybout 1981). As student subjects are expected to fulfill this requirement (e.g., Blair and Zinkhan 2006; Calder et al. 1981; Greenberg 1987), the samples of both, study 1 and study 2, merely consisted of students. However, such a sample structure typically raises questions about the generalizability of results (e.g., Blair and Zinkhan 2006; Gordon, Slade, and Schmitt 1986; Lynch 1982). For this reason, the third study in this section is intended to confirm the external validity of the medium magnitude effect on participation decisions by means of a field experiment with a heterogeneous sample structure.

1.1 Study 1

1.1.1 Participants, Design, and Procedure

As an initial test of the proposed effect of medium magnitude on the likelihood of joining a loyalty program (H1a) study 1 focuses on individuals' preferences between two consequentially equivalent loyalty programs in an airline context. Students who registered online for marketing classes at TU Dortmund University were recruited via e-mail to take part in an online study. The answers of 216 respondents (M_{age} = 24.4 years, 49.5% female) were used for analysis.

As shown in figure 9, the cover story of this study asked participants to imagine that their favorite airline offered two identical programs which solely differed regarding their specification of medium magnitude in terms of low and high. Respondents then were asked to indicate which program they preferred to join.

Figure 9. Loyalty Program Schemes of Study 1

Please imagine that your favorite airline offers the following reward programs for its customers:

Program A	This program credits **1 loyalty point** per flight. After **20 flights** you can redeem your collected **20 loyalty points** for a free flight.
Program B	This program credits **100 loyalty points** per flight. After **20 flights** you can redeem your collected **2,000 loyalty points** for a free flight.

Which program would you prefer to join?

- Program A
- Program B

In accordance with the initial airline example the company's low magnitude program (program A) offered 1 loyalty point for every flight and a free ticket for 20 points, whereas the high magnitude program (program B) credited 100 points per flight and a free flight for 2,000 points. Thus, both programs required the same input (20 paid tickets) for the same outcome (a free ticket). Hence, if the proposed positive effect of medium magnitude on the likelihood of joining a program does not exist, program choices should be equally distributed between the high and low magnitude program, i.e. half of the respondents should choose program A, and the other half should choose program B.

1.1.2 Results

As can be seen in figure 10, more participants (56.9%, 123 of 216 respondents) preferred joining the high magnitude program over the low magnitude program (43.1%, 93 of 216 respondents).

Figure 10. Participation Preferences between High and Low Magnitude Programs

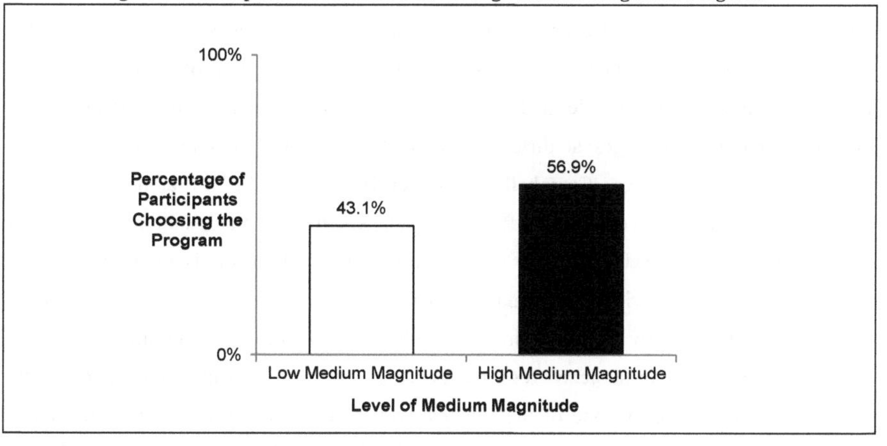

Although the differences in the preference between both programs were relatively small, the detected choice shares are not equally distributed ($\chi^2(1) = 4.17$, $p < .05$). This finding is consistent with H1a and could be considered as preliminary evidence for the proposed medium magnitude effect on participation decisions.

1.2 Study 2

1.2.1 Participants, Design, and Procedure

After study 1 has demonstrated that individuals prefer joining a high magnitude program over a low magnitude program, study 2 focuses on more realistic situations; namely, people's choice between participation and non-participation in a specific loyalty program. Besides testing the predicted positive impact of medium magnitude on the participation likelihood (H1a), this study additionally investigates the extent to which this effect is moderated by dominance between choice alternatives (H2a) which is determined by the advantage of the participation over the non-participation. Students who registered online for marketing classes at TU Dortmund University were recruited via e-mail to take part in this online study. One hundred twenty-three respondents (M_{age} = 23.2 years, 54.5% female) completed the questionnaire and answered control questions correctly.

Study 2 employed a 2 (low versus high medium magnitude) × 2 (low versus high dominance between choice options) full-factorial experimental design. Thus, the constructed experimental treatment conditions covered every possible combination of the levels of both independent variables (Keppel 1973). Such a study design allows the incorporation of interaction effects between the independent variables and, hence, an evaluation if the effect of one variable—e.g., medium magnitude—changes at different levels of the second variable—e.g., dominance between choice options (e.g., Campbell and Stanley 1963; Green 1973; Malhotra 2010). For the purpose of eliminating carry-over effects between experimental manipulations and, thus, to examine the effects of each of the four resulting treatment conditions in isolation (Greenwald 1976), the independent variables were manipulated between-subjects, such that each respondent was confronted with only one experimental condition. In addition, to minimize the risk of systematic differences in subjects' response behavior among treatment groups, participants were randomly assigned to one of the four experimental conditions to ensure equivalence among subjects across different treatments (Keppel 1973; Kirk 2013). Cell sizes ranged from $n = 29$ to $n = 33$, such that groups were of approximately equal size (Hair et al. 2010).[10] Finally, to statistically control for varying responses due to personal differences, individual respondent

[10] If experimental groups are approximately equally sized, i.e.

$$\frac{\text{largest group size}}{\text{smallest group size}} < 1.5,$$

the robustness of the findings of the subsequently employed analysis of covariance is not jeopardized by deviations from normal distribution and variance homogeneity of the dependent variable (Hair et al. 2010).

characteristics which are expected to influence response behavior were measured as well and employed as covariates during analysis (Hair et al. 2010; Kirk 2013; Malhotra 2010).

The cover story used in this experiment asked participants to imagine that they frequently visited a friend living 300 kilometers away and that traveling by train turned out to be the lowest priced alternative for their journeys. In accordance with current market prices, the one way ticket price was indicated with €40. Moreover, participants were told that the fictive railway company which they should imagine to use regularly for their trips operated a loyalty scheme.

1.2.2 Operationalization of Variables

1.2.2.1 Independent Variables

To operationalize the independent variables of medium magnitude and dominance between choice options, novel experimental manipulations were developed. The manipulation of the magnitude of the loyalty program medium was designed based on research by Raghubir and Srivatava (2002) who explored individuals' spending behavior when using foreign currencies in situations where the face value of the foreign currency was either a multiple or a fraction of an equivalent unit of the home currency. Therefore, the magnitude of the program medium was manipulated such that members in the high magnitude conditions earned 100 points for every €10 spent and, thus, the nominal number of issued points constitutes a multiple of the amount spent on the company. Conversely, in the low magnitude conditions, members were credited only 1 point per €10 and, hence, a fraction of their spending.

The dominance between choice options was manipulated by varying the requisite effort for a constant reward (a free ticket) and, consequently, the outcome/effort ratio of the loyalty program under consideration. In the high dominance conditions the travel reward could be redeemed after spending at least €400 (i.e. 10 paid tickets), whereas the low dominance program required a minimum of €1,600 spent on the company (i.e. 40 paid tickets). Thus, depending on the specification of medium magnitude, the free ticket in the low dominance conditions was priced with 160 points and 16,000 points, whereas the price of the reward in the high dominance conditions was indicated with 40 and 4,000 points, respectively. Figure 11 illustrates the resulting loyalty program schemes.

Note that, in the high dominance condition, program enrollment entails an average discount of about 10 percent which should be perceived to be clearly dominant to non-participation which involves no such discount. In contrast, increasing the effort required for redemption from 10 paid tickets to 40 paid tickets corresponds to a mere discount of about 2.5 percent which should result in a more ambiguous dominance structure between participation and non-participation. Thus, while the low dominance programs might lack of convincing reasons to choose participation over non-participation due to an unattractive outcome/effort relation, there is a more decisive argument for preferring participation in the high dominance conditions.

Figure 11. Loyalty Program Schemes of Study 2

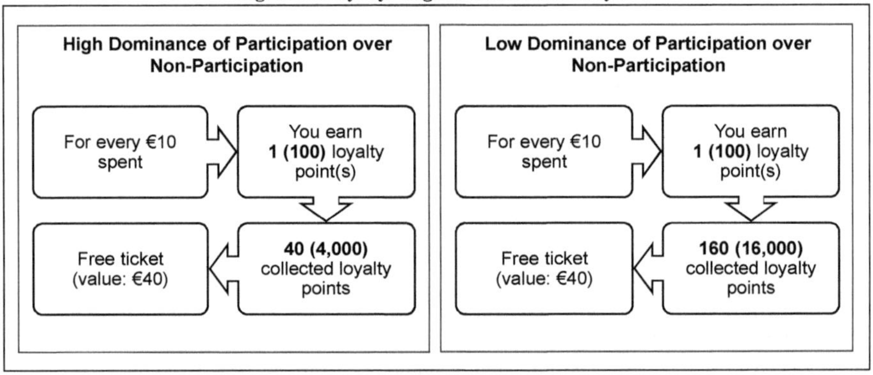

As already stated, according to rational choice theory, the likelihood of joining the program should be solely determined by the outcome/effort ratio of the loyalty scheme under consideration and, thus, since participants in the high dominance conditions have to exert less effort to attain the reward, they should be more likely to participate in the described program than those in the low dominance conditions. Furthermore, since the manipulation of the magnitude of the loyalty program currency merely affects the nominal number of credited points but not their value in real terms, the enrollment likelihood should be, normatively, independent of medium magnitude.

1.2.2.2 Dependent Variable, Manipulation Checks, and Covariates

Next to the presentation of one of the four resulting program schemes, respondents were asked to indicate their intentions to participate in the introduced loyalty program. Therefore, the dependent variable likelihood of joining the program was measured in accordance with Kivetz and Simonson (2002, 2003) with a single item on a seven-point scale ranging from "very unlikely to join this program" (1) to "very likely to join this program" (7).

To confirm that the employed manipulations were adequate operationalizations of their associated variables, participants were asked manipulation-check questions (Perdue and Summers 1986). The perception of medium magnitude was evaluated with the statement "this program offers a large number of points per euro spent" (Bagchi and Lee 2011), whereas dominance between choice options was measured with the items "Participating in this program offers a lot of advantages when compared to non-participation" and "Participating in this program is economically advantageous when compared to non-participation". To control for potential external influences on the likelihood of joining the program, participants evaluated several covariate measures. First, since Taylor and Neslin (2005) showed that customers' price consciousness is positively related to their perception of the importance of loyalty cards, price consciousness may affect loyalty program enrollment as well (Demoulin and Zidda 2009). The construct of price consciousness was measured with three items proposed by Donthu and Garcia (1999). Second, the perceived attractiveness of rewards is expected to affect individuals' participation decisions (Liu and Brock 2009) and, therefore, was also measured (Evanschitzky et al. 2011; Yi and Jeon 2003). Finally, previous research has shown that the number of existing loyalty program memberships is related to new program adoption (e.g., Leenheer et al. 2007; Meyer-Waarden and Benavent 2003). For this reason, participants were asked to indicate the number of loyalty cards permanently in the wallet (Liston-Heyes 2002) an indicator for their general attitude toward loyalty programs. These control variables were assessed after the experiment was completed as the experimental conditions were not expected to influence the scores on these measures (Keppel 1973). Table 13 provides an overview of all measures used in this study.

The adequacy of the employed multi-item scales was evaluated by means of standard quality criteria. More specifically, individual item reliabilities were assessed by an examination of factor loadings—i.e. the correlation between each item and its respective construct—which are generally recommended to exceed the value of .7, such that a minimum of 50 percent of the variance of an item is shared with its respective factor (e.g., Hair et al. 2010; Hulland 1999; Hair, Ringle, and Sarstedt 2011). Cronbach's (1951) alpha scores, which represent the average correlation between items of one construct, served to evaluate internal consistency of the employed measurement models. Alpha scores above .7 are commonly considered acceptable (e.g., Kaplan and Saccuzzo 1982; Murphy and Davidshofer 1988; Nunally 1978). However, since Cronbach's alpha is not an adequate criterion to assess the reliability of two-item scales, measurement models consisting of only two variables were evaluated by means of Spearman Brown coefficients (e.g., Eisinga, te Grotenhuis, and Pelzer 2013; Hulin and Cudeck 2001; Li, Rosenthal, and Rubin 1996) as well as commonly used Pearson correlation coefficients and their associated level of significance (e.g., Posavac et al. 2004; Roehm et al. 2002; Wirtz et al. 2007).

Table 13. Operationalization of Latent Variables (Study 2)

Latent Variables and Items	**Factor Loadings**
Dependent Variable	
Likelihood of Joining the Program	
▪ How likely are you to participate in this loyalty program? ("very unlikely to join this program"/"very likely to join this program")	-
Manipulation Checks	
Medium Magnitude	
▪ This program offers a large number of points per euro spent.	-
Dominance Between Choice Options (ρ = .83; r = .71, p < .01)	
▪ Participating in this program offers a lot of advantages when compared to non-participation.	.86
▪ Participating in this program is economically advantageous when compared to non-participation.	.86
Control Variables	
Perceived Attractiveness of Rewards (ρ = .80; r = .66, p < .01)	
▪ The proposed rewards have high cash value.	.91
▪ The proposed rewards are what I want.	.91
Price Consciousness (α = . 79)	
▪ When shopping, I often find myself checking the prices.	.87
▪ One can save a lot of money by shopping around for bargains.	.80
▪ I usually purchase items on sale only.	.85
Attitude toward Loyalty Programs	
▪ How many loyalty cards do you have permanently in your wallet?	-

Note: All measures not indicated otherwise were assessed on seven-point scales anchored by "strongly disagree" (1) and "strongly agree" (7).

As can be seen in table 13, exploratory factory analyses revealed factor loadings above the required threshold for all items. In addition, calculation of alpha scores, as well as Spearman Brown coefficients and item correlations, respectively, confirm the internal consistency of all measurement models. Thus, for further analysis, responses to multiple items of the same construct were averaged into a single index.

1.2.3 Results

1.2.3.1 Manipulation Checks

The appropriateness of the developed manipulations was assessed by means of two analyses of variance (ANOVAs) which examine whether variations in the manipulation check measures of both independent variables are predominantly caused by their corresponding manipulation and preferably not by the manipulation of the other variable (Perdue and Summers 1986).

An ANOVA with the perceived number of points earned per euro spent revealed a main effect of the specification of the program's medium magnitude ($F(1, 119) = 49.40, p < .01$) and a significant interaction between medium magnitude and dominance ($F(1, 119) = 3.65, p < .10$). Respondents' ratings of the perception of medium magnitude confirmed that the manipulation of this independent variable worked as intended. As expected, participants who were confronted with a high magnitude program were aware that they earned a large number of points per euro spent on the company relative to subjects in the low magnitude conditions ($M_{\text{mm-low}} = 2.60$ versus $M_{\text{mm-high}} = 4.24$, $t(121) = 6.93$, $p < .01$). A closer examination of the potential confounding effect of the unintended interaction revealed that—despite its significance—the number of earned points was perceived as higher in both high magnitude conditions than in both low magnitude conditions. Hence, the manipulation of medium magnitude can be considered satisfactory.

An ANOVA with perceived advantage of participation over non-participation elicited a significant main effect of the dominance manipulation ($F(1, 119) = 15.62, p < .01$). Specifically, the variation of requisite effort to redeem a reward affected the perceived dominance between choice options in the desired direction; i.e. increasing the prices of the rewards from 40 to 160 points respectively from 4,000 to 16,000 points led to significantly lower perceived advantage of participation over non-participation ($M_{\text{dom-low}} = 4.24$ versus $M_{\text{dom-high}} = 5.26$, $t(121) = 3.80$, $p < .01$). However, the main effect of medium magnitude ($F(1, 119) = 3.65, p < .10$) as well as the dominance × medium magnitude interaction ($F(1, 119) = 3.65$, $p < .10$) were also significant. Nonetheless, the perceived dominance of participation over non-participation was higher in both high dominance conditions than in both low dominance conditions, confirming an appropriate operationalization of this independent variable as well.

1.2.3.2 Hypotheses

The proposed hypotheses were tested using an analysis of covariance (ANCOVA) which adjusts the results for differences among respondents using the measured control variable values and, thereby, reduces the proportion of unexplained variance of the dependent variable (e.g., Hair et al. 2010; Keppel 1973; Kirk 2013). The conducted ANCOVA with perceived attractiveness of rewards ($F(1, 116) = 15.99$, $p < .01$), price consciousness ($F(1, 116) = 3.06$, $p < .10$), and attitude toward loyalty programs ($F(1, 116) = 10.09$, $p < .01$) used as covariates revealed significant main effects of medium magnitude ($F(1, 116) = 5.85$, $p < .05$) and dominance between choice options ($F(1, 116) = 11.03$, $p < .05$) on the likelihood of joining the program. In addition, a significant dominance × medium magnitude interaction emerged ($F(1, 116) = 4.17$, $p < .05$). These results are summarized in table 14.

Table 14. ANCOVA Results of Study 2

	F	*p*
Main Effects		
Medium Magnitude	5.85	< .05
Dominance Between Choice Options	11.03	< .01
Interaction Effect		
Medium Magnitude × Dominance Between Choice Options	4.17	< .05
Covariates		
Perceived Attractiveness of Rewards	15.99	< .01
Price Consciousness	3.06	< .10
Attitude toward Loyalty Programs	10.09	< .01

In support of the proposed medium magnitude effect (H1a), increasing the magnitude of the program currency had a positive effect on the likelihood of joining the program; Respondents in the high magnitude conditions were more likely to sign up for the described program than those in the low magnitude groups ($M_{\text{mm-high}} = 5.05$ versus $M_{\text{mm-low}} = 4.47$, $t(121) = 1.71$, $p < .10$). In addition, though not explicitly hypothesized, dominance between choice options had positive effect on the likelihood of joining the program, such that the higher advantage program was associated with a higher participation likelihood ($M_{\text{dom-high}} = 5.33$) than the low advantage program ($M_{\text{dom-low}} = 4.21$, $t(121) = 3.40$, $p < .01$). This finding is consistent with the positive relationship between the outcome/input ratio of a loyalty program and participation likelihood described in equation 12.

Considering the interaction between medium magnitude and dominance between choice options, when respondents were told that the travel reward required the accumulation of 40 paid tickets (i.e. low dominance of participation over non-participation), increasing the program currency's magnitude led to a significant increase in the respondents' reported likelihood of joining the program ($M_{\text{mm-high}} = 4.82$ versus $M_{\text{mm-low}} = 3.52$, $t(60) = 2.68$, $p < .01$, see figure 12).

Figure 12. The Effect of Medium Magnitude and Dominance between Choice Options on the Likelihood of Joining the Program

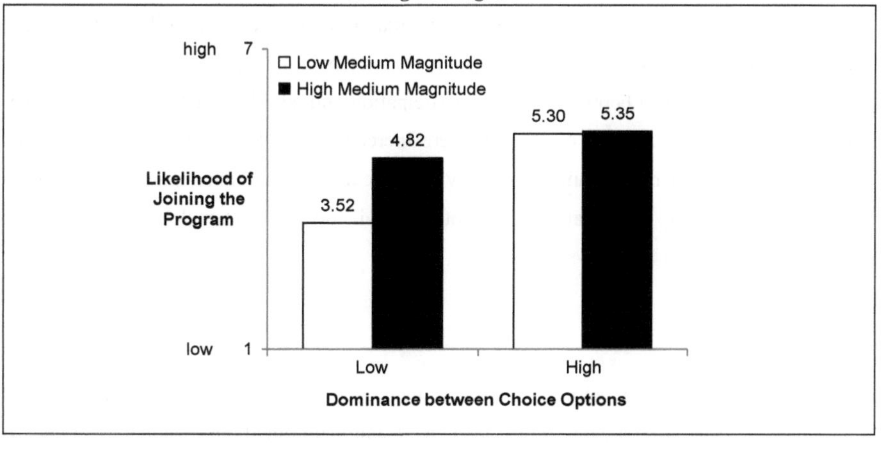

Conversely, when respondents were told that the free ticket required only 10 paid tickets (i.e. high dominance of participation over non-participation), the enrollment likelihood remained unaffected by variations of the specification of medium magnitude ($M_{\text{mm-high}} = 5.35$ versus $M_{\text{mm-low}} = 5.30$, $t(59) = .129$, n.s.). Hence, in line with hypothesis 2a, high dominance between choice options constitutes a boundary condition of the effect of medium magnitude on participation decisions.

1.3 Study 3

1.3.1 Participants, Design, and Procedure

The purpose of study 3 is to replicate the positive effect of medium magnitude on participation decisions (H1a) with a heterogeneous sample structure in a different context and, thus, to confirm its external validity. The study was conducted as part of the open house presentation of TU Dortmund University. At the department of marketing, which is located on the fifth floor in a university building on campus, two short introductions in marketing—at 11 a.m. and 2 p.m.—were held. Each presentation was accompanied with a stairs climbing bonus campaign which involved a program medium.

Visitors in the low medium magnitude condition at 11 a.m. were told that the bonus campaign offered one bonus dollar which could be redeemed on the fifth floor for a chocolate egg. In addition, when using the stairs instead of the elevator to reach the department they would earn one additional dollar per floor resulting in a maximum of six bonus dollars which could be redeemed for more precious sweets. In contrast, visitors in the high magnitude condition at 2 p.m. were offered 100 bonus dollars for participation and additional 100 bonus dollars per floor. Accordingly, the prices of rewards were increased by a factor of 100. Prior to each presentation two student assistants informed visitors next to the building about the presentation and the stairs climbing bonus campaign. In total, 106 visitors (55.7% female) were approached and their choices used for analysis.

1.3.2 Results

Of the 51 visitors who were approached in the low medium magnitude condition, 45.1 percent (23 subjects) decided to take part in the introduced stairs climbing bonus campaign and got to the fifth floor—either by using the elevator or the stairs—to receive their rewards. In contrast, of the 55 visitors who were informed about the high magnitude campaign, 81.8 percent (45 subjects) decided to participate. Thus, visitors who encountered the high magnitude program exhibited a significantly higher participation rate than visitors exposed to the low magnitude campaign ($\chi^2(1) = 15.52, p < .01$); suggesting that the positive effect on participation decisions (H1a) also holds in a different context (see figure 13). In addition, visitors' gender had no effect on the choice between participation and non-participation in the bonus campaign ($\chi^2(1) = 1.65$, n.s.).

Figure 13. The Effect of Medium Magnitude on Participation Rate and Exerted Effort

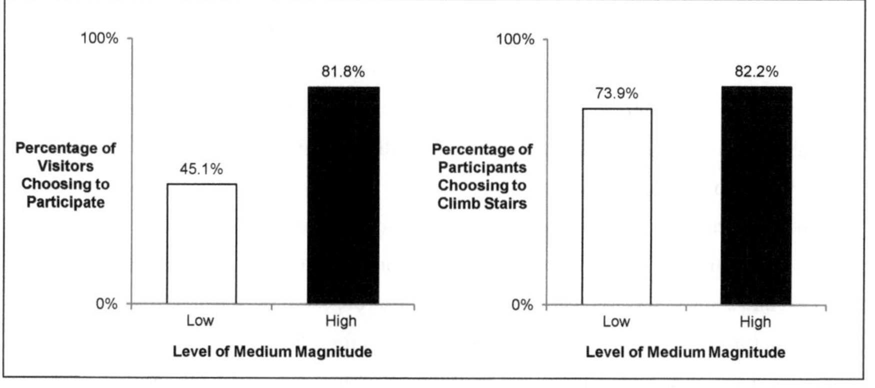

Moreover, the high magnitude program exhibited a marginally higher percentage of subjects who chose climbing the stairs instead of using the elevator to reach the marketing department. Whereas 82.2 percent of the participants (37 of 45) in the high magnitude condition used the stairs to collect more bonus dollars, 73.9 percent of the participants (17 of 23) in the low magnitude condition engaged in the more effortful option. However, a one-tailed Fisher's (1954) exact test[11] reveals that these differences are not statistically significant ($p = .31$).

[11] Fisher's exact test was chosen instead of a χ^2-test for two reasons. First, the number of participants between the low and high magnitude condition is unbalanced and, second, a χ^2-test is not suitable when the expected values in any of the contingency table's cells are below 5 as is the case in this study (e.g., Agresti, Wackerly, and Boyett 1979; Everitt 1992; Woodward 2014).

1.4 Discussion

The purpose of the study series in this section was to confirm the proposed positive effect of medium magnitude in the participation decision context. With regards to the formal description of participation decisions (see equation 12), the programs under consideration in study 1 merely differed regarding their level of medium magnitude, i.e. m^{low} and m^{high}, which solely influences the value of loyalty points in nominal but not in real terms. Hence, the specification of a program medium's magnitude should be irrelevant and people should base their decision exclusively on the comparison of outcome/input ratios of both programs with the result that—due to equivalent outcome/input ratios of the high and low magnitude program—choices between both programs should be equally distributed. However, study 1 supports the assumption that individuals systematically overvalue the nominal number of credited points such that the perceived values $v(m^{low})$ and $v(m^{high})$ become unequal, and, people are more likely to participate in a high magnitude program than in a low magnitude program. In addition, study 1 rules out that the medium magnitude effect on participation decisions has to be solely ascribed to biased anchoring and adjustment processes. The description of the choice problem in this study already informed participants about the absolute effort required for redemption (i.e. 20 paid tickets for a free ticket) such that a mental derivation of the program's outcome/input ratio by means of the program medium—which might be subject to an inaccurate anchoring and adjustment process—was not necessary.

In addition to showing the medium magnitude effect on participation decisions, study 2 also reveals a boundary condition. While the positive effect of medium magnitude on the likelihood of joining the program is observed for programs with a relatively low outcome/input ratio and, hence, a low advantage of participation, a high dominance of participation over non-participation diminishes the relative weight w of incorporating the irrelevant specification of medium magnitude into decision-making, such that participation decisions remain unaffected by variations of the program medium's magnitude. This suggests that, if the outcome/input ratio of a loyalty program is low, an exclusive focus on this attribute does not provide adequate reasons for enrollment decisions and individuals tend to use the magnitude of the program currency as a cue to infer the attractiveness of a loyalty program, such that participating in a high magnitude program becomes more likely. In contrast, if a program's outcome/input ratio leads to a clear dominance of participation over non-participation, the irrelevant magnitude of the program medium loses weight.

Finally, study 3 rules out that the medium magnitude effect has to be solely ascribed to context or sample structure by providing a more realistic test of this phenomenon involving real participation decisions with actual, more or less effortful, consequences. In sum, the studies in this section highlight that the medium magnitude effect in the participation decision context is robust among different types of analysis and study designs, ranging from a simple decision problem (study 1) over a scenario-based experiment (study 2) to a field experiment in a different context (study 3).

2 The Impact of Medium Magnitude on Redemption Decisions

The following series of studies examines the medium magnitude effect in the redemption decision context. More specifically, the purpose of the subsequently documented investigations is to empirically test the proposed negative effect of the magnitude of a loyalty program medium on the likelihood of redeeming accumulated points (H1b) and to provide support for the expected moderating role of dominance between choice options (H2b). For ease of discussion, recall equation 14 which formally describes the likelihood of choosing redemption over non-redemption:

$$L_{redeem}^{low/high}\ (r;\ r,\ nr) = (1 - w) \cdot v\left(\frac{Outcome_r}{Input_r}\right) + w \cdot v\left(-m^{low/high}\right). \qquad (14)$$

The subsequent examinations address its three components; namely, the perceived value of the nominal number of requisite points for redemption in a low magnitude program—i.e. $v\left(-m^{low}\right)$—and in a high magnitude program—i.e. $v\left(-m^{high}\right)$—respectively, as well as scheme members' perceptions of the outcome/input ratio of the reward under consideration and the relative weight parameter w which reflects the extent to which the perceived value of the nominal number of points provides a reason for redemption decisions

For the empirical test of the proposed hypotheses the following procedure applies. Study 4 is intended to provide preliminary evidence for the negative effect of the magnitude of a loyalty program medium on redemption decisions by analyzing redemption preferences among high and low magnitude designs. Thus, this study concentrates on differences in the perceived value of the nominal number of points required for redemption between programs with currencies of different magnitudes. In a next step, study 5 focusses on an investigation of the hypothesized effect of dominance between choice options in the redemption decision context and, thus, the relative weight w of incorporating the irrelevant nominal number of requisite points into redemption decisions. Finally, study 6 aims to confirm the external validity of the medium magnitude effect on redemption decisions by means of a survey among loyalty program members' perceptions of and behavior in real-world loyalty programs.

2.1 Study 4

2.1.1 Participants, Design, and Procedure

The proposed effect of medium magnitude on the likelihood of redeeming accumulated points (H1b) was initially tested using a simple choice problem in the redemption decision context. Students who registered online for marketing classes at TU Dortmund University were recruited via e-mail to take part in this study. The answers of 187 respondents (M_{age} = 23.0 years, 37.4% female) were used for analysis.

The study scenario asked participants to imagine that they were participating in two frequent flyer programs in which they already accumulated enough points to redeem a free flight. In addition, respondents were told that they were planning their next trip and asked to indicate in which of the two programs they preferred to redeem a free ticket. Both programs solely differed regarding their specification of medium magnitude in terms of high and low and, thus, in the number of requisite points for redemption. In accordance with study 1, the low magnitude program (program A) offered 1 point for every flight and required 20 points for the free ticket, whereas the high magnitude program (program B) credited 100 points per flight and required 2,000 points for the flight reward. Figure 14 illustrates the choice problem of study 4.

Figure 14. Loyalty Program Schemes of Study 4

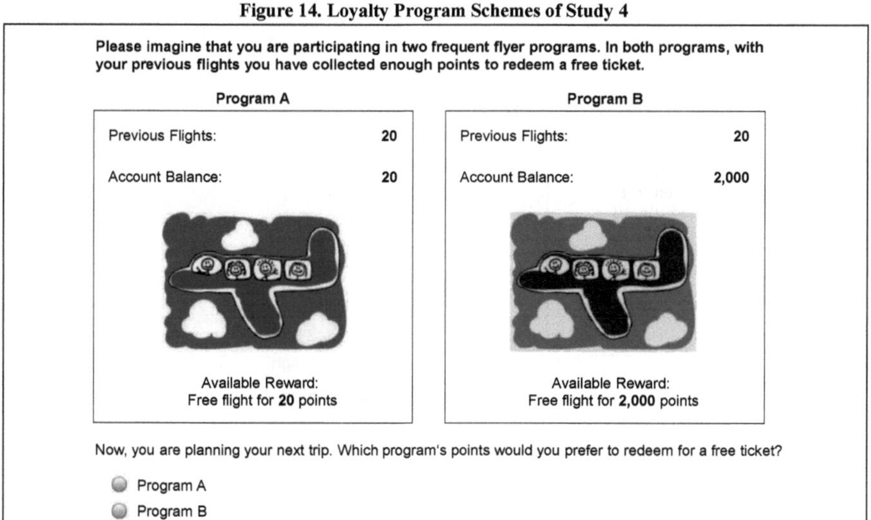

Although both program rewards differ regarding the nominal value of loyalty points required for redemption, the effort of accumulating these points (i.e. 20 paid tickets) was identical among them. Hence, if the proposed negative effect of medium magnitude on the likelihood of redeeming accumulated points would not exist, redemption preferences should be equally distributed among the low and high magnitude program; i.e. half of the respondents should choose to redeem their collected points in program A and the other half should decide to redeem their ticket in program B.

2.1.2 Results

The results are illustrated in figure 15. As can be seen, more participants (71.7%, 134 of 187 respondents) preferred to redeem their accumulated points in the low magnitude program instead of in the high magnitude program (28.3%, 53 of 187 respondents). Further analyses revealed that these preference shares are significantly not equally distributed ($\chi^2(1) = 35.09$, $p < .01$). This finding provides preliminary evidence for the expected negative medium magnitude effect on redemption decisions (H1b).

Figure 15. Redemption Preferences between High and Low Magnitude Programs

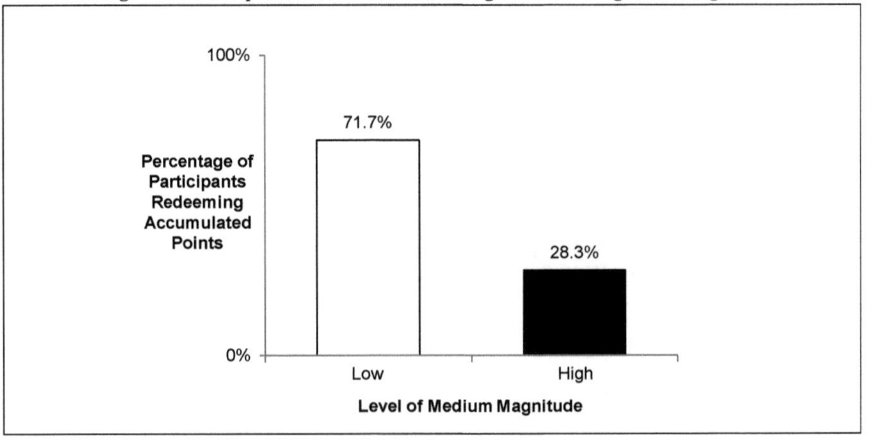

2.2 Study 5

2.2.1 Participants, Design, and Procedure

Study 4 has shown that individuals prefer paying rewards with low magnitude program currencies rather than with high magnitude currencies. However, since people are usually not confronted with the choice between redemption in different programs, study 5 addresses a more common consumer choice problem; namely, situations where program members have to decide whether to redeem or to save their accrued points in a specific program. Aside from testing the proposed negative impact of medium magnitude on the likelihood of redeeming accumulated points (H1b), this study additionally investigates if dominance between choice options can diminish this effect in a way similar to the participation decision context (H2b). The answers of 124 (M_{age} = 23.9 years, 50.0% female) students who were invited via e-mail to take part in this online study were used for analysis. Study 5 was designed as a 2 (low versus high medium magnitude) × 2 (low versus high dominance between choice options) full-factorial, between-subjects experiment. Participants were randomly assigned to one of the four experimental groups. Cell sizes ranged from $n = 30$ to $n = 32$.

Using the cover story of study 2, the study scenarios asked participants to imagine that they frequently traveled by train to visit a friend who lived 300 kilometers away. The one way ticket price for this journey was indicated with €30. Moreover, respondents should imagine that they were participating in a loyalty program of the fictive railway company that they regularly used for their trips. Participants were additionally told that they exactly accumulated enough points to redeem a single ticket for their next trip. In addition to the number of points required for a one way ticket, information about the requisite number of points for a round-trip ticket was provided, such that non-redemption was also plausible.

2.2.2 Operationalization of Variables

2.2.2.1 Independent Variables

Similar to the railway company's program schemes used in study 2, the magnitude of the program medium was manipulated such that members in the high magnitude conditions required 3,000 points for the free one way ticket, while earning 100 points for every €10 spent. In contrast, in the low magnitude conditions members were credited only 1 point per €10 and, consequently, could redeem a free single ticket after accruing 30 points.

The second independent variable, dominance between choice options (i.e. between redemption and non-redemption), was manipulated by varying number of points required for a free round-trip ticket (see figure 16). In the low dominance conditions the free round-trip ticket price was exactly twice as high as the number of requisite points for the one way ticket reward. Hence, since logically a round-trip ticket equals two single tickets, participants should be more or less indifferent between redemption and non-redemption. In this case, the magnitude of the prices of rewards might serve as an additional justification for redemption decisions. In high dominance conditions, in contrast, the round-trip ticket reward was cheaper than the price of two single tickets, such that non-redemption—in particular, in the form of continuing the saving process toward future redemption—should clearly dominate current redemption with the consequence that medium magnitude might not be incorporated into decision-making.

Figure 16. Prices of Rewards in Study 5

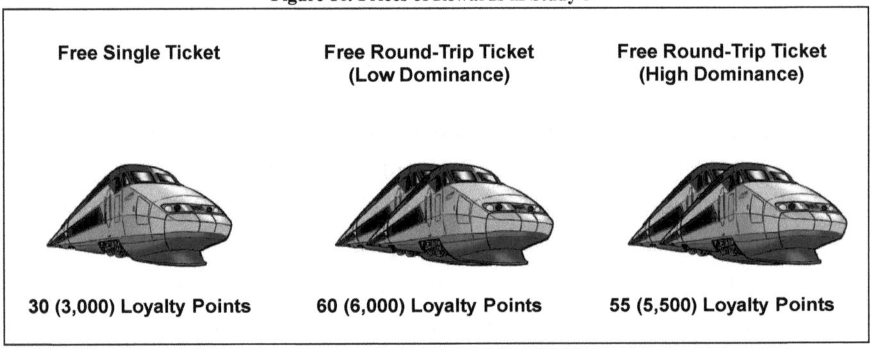

2.2.2.2 Dependent Variable, Manipulation Checks, and Covariates

The dependent variable likelihood of redeeming accumulated points for the one way ticket was measured with a single item on a seven-point scale ranging from "very unlikely to redeem the reward" (1) to "very likely to redeem the reward" (7). To assess the performance of the manipulations, manipulation-check questions were adopted from study 2. The perception of medium magnitude was evaluated with the statement "this program requires a large number of points to redeem a reward", whereas the dominance perceptions between redemption and non-redemption were measured with the items "Redemption of accumulated points offers a lot of advantages compared to non-redemption" and "Redemption of accumulated points is economically advantageous compared to non-redemption" (1 = strongly disagree, 7 = strongly agree). In accordance with study 2, to control for potential external influences on the likelihood of redeeming accumulated points, price consciousness, perceived attractiveness of rewards, and attitude towards loyalty programs were also measured.

Table 15 provides an overview of the used measurement models and associated quality criteria. Due to high scores on the reliability measures (i.e. Cronbach's alpha, Spearman-Brown and correlation coefficients, as well as factor loadings), responses to multiple items of the same construct were averaged to index values which were used for further analysis.

Table 15. Operationalization of Latent Variables (Study 5)

Latent Variables and Items	Factor Loadings
Dependent Variable	
Likelihood of Redeeming Accumulated Points	
▪ How likely are you to redeem your accumulated points for the free single ticket? ("very unlikely to redeem the reward"/"very likely to redeem the reward")	-
Manipulation Checks	
Medium Magnitude	
▪ This program requires a large number of points to redeem a reward.	-
Dominance Between Choice Options (ρ = .72; r = .56, p < .01)	
▪ Redemption of accumulated points offers a lot of advantages compared to non-redemption.	.88
▪ Redemption of accumulated points is economically advantageous compared to non-redemption.	.88
Control Variables	
Perceived Attractiveness of Rewards	
▪ The proposed program rewards are very attractive.	-
Price Consciousness (α = . 81)	
▪ When shopping, I often find myself checking the prices.	.79
▪ One can save a lot of money by shopping around for bargains.	.84
▪ I usually purchase items on sale only.	.92
Attitude toward Loyalty Programs	
▪ How many loyalty cards do you have permanently in your wallet?	-

Note: All measures not indicated otherwise were assessed on seven-point scales anchored by "strongly disagree" (1) and "strongly agree" (7).

2.2.3 Results

2.2.3.1 Manipulation Checks

An ANOVA with points required for redemption elicited a significant main effect of the manipulation of the magnitude of the program medium ($F(1, 120) = 4.26$, $p < .05$) and a significant interaction between medium magnitude and dominance ($F(1, 120) = 2.95$, $p < .10$). However, participants exposed with a high magnitude design recognized that redeeming the single ticket required a larger number of points relative to those confronted with a low magnitude program ($M_{\text{mm-low}} = 3.87$ versus $M_{\text{mm-high}} = 4.44$, $t(122) = 2.02$, $p < .05$). Hence, despite the unintended significant interaction effect, the manipulation of medium magnitude can be considered satisfactory.

Considering the effectiveness of the dominance manipulation, an ANOVA elicited significant main effects of dominance ($F(1, 120) = 14.29$, $p < .01$) and medium magnitude ($F(1, 120) = 8.18$, $p < .01$). As expected, lowering the prices of the round-trip ticket from 60 to 55 respectively from 6,000 to 5,500 led to a significant decrease of the perceived advantage of redemption over non-redemption ($M_{\text{dom-low}} = 3.72$ versus $M_{\text{dom-high}} = 2.67$, $t(122) = 3.73$, $p < .01$). Thus, this manipulation created the expected perception of dominance structures between choice options.

2.2.3.2 Hypotheses

An ANCOVA with the perceived attractiveness of rewards ($F(1, 117) = .64$, n.s.), price consciousness ($F(1, 117) = .33$, n.s.), and attitude toward loyalty programs ($F(1, 117) = .78$, n.s.) used as covariates elicited significant main effects of medium magnitude ($F(1, 117) = 4.09$, $p < .05$) and dominance between choice options ($F(1, 117) = 30.72$, $p < .01$) on the likelihood of redeeming accumulated points. Moreover, a significant dominance × medium magnitude interaction ($F(1, 117) = 2.89$, $p < .10$) emerged. These results are summarized in table 16.

In support of H1b, medium magnitude had a negative effect on the likelihood of redeeming accumulated points, such that participants in the low magnitude conditions were more likely to redeem the single ticket ($M_{\text{mm-low}} = 4.33$) than participants in the high magnitude conditions ($M_{\text{mm-high}} = 3.56$, $t(122) = 2.03$, $p < .05$). In addition, an increasing dominance of future redemption over current redemption decreases the likelihood of redeeming the single ticket ($M_{\text{dom-low}} = 4.89$ versus $M_{\text{dom-high}} = 3.02$, $t(122) = 5.36$, $p < .01$).

Table 16. ANCOVA Results of Study 5

	F	*p*
Main Effects		
Medium Magnitude	4.09	<. 05
Dominance Between Choice Options	30.72	< .01
Interaction Effect		
Medium Magnitude × Dominance Between Choice Options	2.89	< .10
Covariates		
Perceived Attractiveness of Rewards	.64	n.s.
Price Consciousness	.33	n.s.
Attitude toward Loyalty Programs	.78	n.s.

Moreover, hypothesis 2b suggests that the difference in the likelihood of redeeming accumulated points between the low and the high magnitude condition will be significant when dominance between choice options is low but will be reduced when comparing both high dominance conditions (see figure 17).

Figure 17. The Effect of Medium Magnitude and Dominance between Choice Options on the Likelihood of Redeeming Accumulated Points

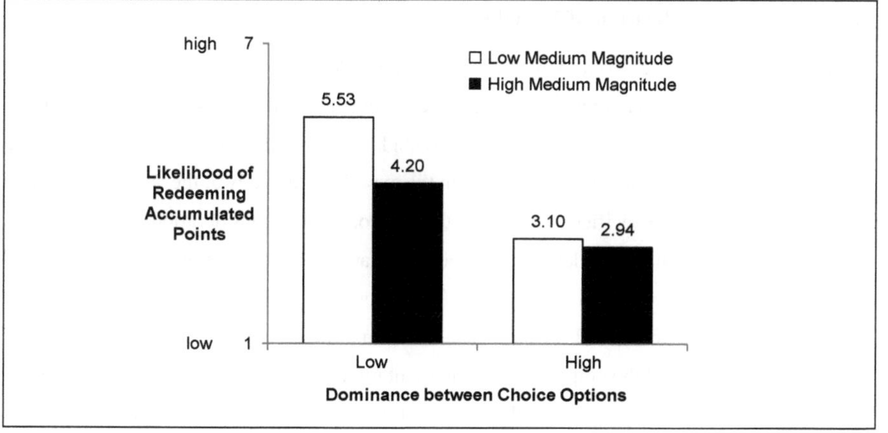

A closer examination of the significant interaction effect revealed that—in line with H2b—medium magnitude indeed had a negative effect on the likelihood of redeeming accumulated points in case of low dominance ($M_{\text{mm-low}} = 5.53$ versus $M_{\text{mm-high}} = 4.20$, $t(60) = 2.62$, $p < .05$) but not when it was high ($M_{\text{mm-low}} = 3.10$ versus $M_{\text{mm-high}} = 2.94$, $t(60) = .35$, n.s.). Hence, as shown in figure 17, similar to the participation decision context, a clear dominance structure between choice options stashes the medium magnitude effect on redemption decisions.

2.3 Study 6

2.3.1 Participants, Design, and Procedure

To provide support for the external validity of the experimental findings on the effect of medium magnitude on redemption decisions, additional data about consumers' perceptions of and redemption behavior in real-world loyalty programs was collected by means of a paper-and-pencil survey. As part of an introduction course to academic research and writing, students were asked to accomplish the data collection task. In total, 520 questionnaires were returned. The answers of 447 participants ($M_{\text{age}} = 30.9$ years, $SD_{\text{age}} = 12.7$, 55.9% female) who indicated that they were participating in at least one loyalty program were used for analysis. Besides variance in respondents' age, participants differed regarding their profession (46.5% students, 42.7% employees or self-employed, and 10.7% retired, homemakers, or unemployed).

2.3.2 Operationalization of Variables

Survey participants were asked to evaluate the loyalty program which they were most familiar with using—with one exception—the same scales as in study 5; the measurement model of the likelihood of redeeming accumulated points was slightly modified. Instead of merely assessing the likelihood of redemption as was the case in the experimental study 5, the scale item used in this consumer survey specified the redemption period under consideration at six months. Besides measures of the dependent and independent variables, the questionnaire also included scales to assess the control variables of perceived attractiveness of rewards, price consciousness, attitude toward loyalty programs, and duration of membership. Table 17 provides an overview of the employed measurement models and—where possible—associated quality criteria. In accordance with the above studies, responses to multi-item scales were averaged for further analysis.

Table 17. Operationalization of Latent Variables (Study 6)

Latent Variables and Items	Factor Loadings
Dependent Variable	
Likelihood of Redeeming Accumulated Points	
▪ How likely are you to redeem your accumulated points for a reward within the next six months? ("very unlikely"/"very likely")	-
Independent Variables	
Medium Magnitude	
▪ This program requires a large number of points to redeem a reward.	-
Dominance Between Choice Options (ρ = .83; r = .71, p < .01)	
▪ Redemption of accumulated points offers a lot of advantages compared to non-redemption.	.92
▪ Redemption of accumulated points is economically advantageous compared to non-redemption.	.92
Control Variables	
Perceived Attractiveness of Rewards (ρ = .56; r = .39, p < .01)	
▪ The proposed program rewards have high cash value.	.84
▪ The proposed program rewards are what I want.	.84
Price Consciousness (α = . 79)	
▪ When shopping, I often find myself checking the prices.	.86
▪ One can save a lot of money by shopping around for bargains.	.80
▪ I usually purchase items on sale only.	.96
Attitude toward Loyalty Programs	
▪ How many loyalty cards do you have permanently in your wallet?	-
Duration of Membership	
▪ How long have you been participating in the program?	-

Note: All measures not indicated otherwise were assessed on seven-point scales anchored by "strongly disagree" (1) and "strongly agree" (7).

2.3.3 Results

To provide evidence on the proposed effect of medium magnitude on redemption decisions and the moderating impact of dominance structures between choice options, regression analysis was used with all variables zero centered to reduce multicollinearity (highest variance inflation factor[12] = 1.215) between the interaction term and its components (Aiken and West 1991).

The likelihood of redeeming accumulated points was regressed on the perceptions of medium magnitude, dominance of redemption over non-redemption, and their two-way interaction as well as the control variables of attractiveness of rewards, price consciousness, duration of membership, and attitude toward loyalty programs ($F(7, 439) = 32.25$, $p < .01$, $R^2 = .34$). The results of the estimation of regression coefficients appear in table 18. Both the first-order effect of medium magnitude ($\beta = -.11$, $t = 2.90$, $p < .01$) and dominance of redemption of non-redemption ($\beta = .47$, $t = 11.09$, $p < .01$) turned out to be significant. Moreover, as expected, a significant medium magnitude × dominance interaction emerged ($\beta = .08$, $t = 1.99$, $p < .05$).

Table 18. Regression Results of Study 6

	β	*t*	*p*
Main Effects			
Medium Magnitude	−.11	2.90	< .01
Dominance between Choice Options	.47	11.09	< .01
Interaction Effect			
Medium Magnitude × Dominance between Choice Options	.08	1.99	< .05
Covariates			
Perceived Attractiveness of Rewards	.16	3.84	< .01
Price Consciousness	.03	.68	n.s.
Duration of Participation	−.07	1.67	< .10
Attitude toward Loyalty Programs	.07	1.66	< .10

12 The variance inflation factor is a measure for the degree of multicollinearity among independent variables providing an index which reflects how much the variance of an estimated regression coefficient is increased due to shared variance. A high extent of multicollinearity—holding the risk of biased parameter estimates—is indicated by high values on this measure (e.g., Hair et al. 2010). Recommended upper thresholds range from 10 (e.g., Gujarati 2003; Kleinbaum, Kupper, and Muller 1988; Verbeek 2012) to a more strict cutoff of 5 (e.g., Hair et al. 2010, 2011).

To better understand the form of the interaction, the simple effect of medium magnitude was computed for low and high dominance groups separately. Therefore, the sample's median of dominance of redemption over non-redemption (5.00) was used to separate low (< 5.00, $M_{\text{dom-low}} = 3.33$, $n = 220$) from high (≥ 5.00, $M_{\text{dom-high}} = 6.04$, $n = 227$) dominance groups. In line with study 5, the results of these analyses revealed that medium magnitude only reduced the likelihood of redeeming accumulated points in case of low dominance ($\beta = -.20$, $t = 3.01$, $p < .01$) and not when dominance was high ($\beta = -.06$, $t = .97$, n.s.), such that the effect of medium magnitude disappeared with increasing dominance between choice options.

Finally, because the measurements of all variables were taken from a single data source, common method variance might influence some of the evidenced relations (Podsakoff et al. 2003). To test for the potential existence of such a common method bias, Harman's (1976) single-factor test was applied. Therefore, an exploratory factor analysis with all indicators incorporated in the above analysis was conducted. The test indicates a high amount of common variance if either a single factor or one general factor emerges which accounts for the majority of covariance among the variables. However, the results of the conducted factor analysis revealed a multi-factorial variable structure with the first factor accounting for only 20 percent of the overall variance; ruling out biased results due to common method variance (Podsakoff and Organ 1986; Podsakoff et al. 2003).

2.4 Discussion

The studies in this section focused on situations where loyalty program members have to decide whether or not to redeem a reward. Considering equation 14, the programs under consideration in study 4 merely differed regarding their level of medium magnitude solely affecting the nominal number of points required to redeem the offered rewards, but not their real, i.e. effort adjusted, prices. Hence, normatively, members should not be misled by irrelevant nominal prices of rewards, but rather should base their redemption decisions on the outcome/input ratios of the offered rewards. However, study 4 confirms the assumption that individuals systematically overvalue the nominal number of points required to redeem a reward, such that the perceived values of low and high magnitude prices of rewards—formally, $v(-m^{low})$ and $v(-m^{high})$—become unequal, and, people are more likely to redeem accumulated points in a low magnitude program than in a high magnitude program. In other words, this finding suggests that high magnitude prices are perceived as more expensive and, thus, result in a less pronounced willingness to spend high magnitude currencies. Again, the medium magnitude effect cannot be exclusively ascribed to biased anchoring and adjustment processes. Since the description of the choice problem in study 4 informed participants about the absolute effort required for redemption (i.e. 20 paid tickets for a free ticket), a mental derivation of the rewards' real costs by means of the program medium was not required.

Besides the negative main effect of medium magnitude on redemption behavior, study 5 also confirms the proposed boundary condition. While the negative effect of medium magnitude on the likelihood of redeeming accumulated points is strongly pronounced when dominance between redemption and non-redemption is low, dominance between these choice options diminishes the relative weight w of incorporating the irrelevant specification of medium magnitude into decision-making, such that redemption decisions remain unaffected by medium magnitude. Hence, if the dominance structure between choice options does not provide convincing reasons for redemption decisions, individuals tend to use medium magnitude as a cue to infer the attractiveness of redemption, such that redemption in a low magnitude program becomes more likely. In contrast, in case of a clear dominance between redemption and non-redemption, the irrelevant level of medium magnitude becomes less important for redemption decisions.

Finally, the purpose of study 6 was to confirm the external validity of the proposed medium magnitude effect on redemption decisions by investigating real-world loyalty programs. In addition, this study points out that the effect of dominance structures on the relative weight parameter works in two directions. Whereas the manipulation of dominance in study 5 was intended to enhance dominance of non-redemption over redemption, study 6, conversely, reveals that the medium magnitude effect also attenuates if redemption dominates non-redemption. In summary, in particular the purposeful composition of above studies by selecting different survey designs and methods of analysis substantiate the robustness of the identified medium magnitude effect on redemption decisions and its boundary condition.

3 The Impact of Medium Magnitude on Purchase Decisions

Besides participation and redemption decisions, different specifications of the magnitude of a loyalty program medium were also hypothesized to alter members' purchase decisions. This section addresses consumers' choice among products of different quality and prices. Specifically, the purpose of the following three studies is to investigate the predicted positive medium magnitude effect on the likelihood of buying a premium product instead of a standard product (H3a) and, furthermore, to provide support for the proposed moderating influence of dominance structures between the available choice options (H4a). Formally, the following examinations focus on each parameter contained in the already introduced equation 17,

$$L_{buy}^{low/high}(pp;\, pp,\, sp) = (1-w)\cdot v\left(\frac{Outcome_{pp}}{Input_{pp}} - \frac{Outcome_{sp}}{Input_{sp}}\right) + w\cdot v\left(m_{pp}^{low/high} - m_{sp}^{low/high}\right), \qquad (17)$$

which describes the likelihood of choosing a premium product over a standard product as a function of the perceived difference in outcome/input ratios between the premium and the standard product under consideration, the perceived difference in the nominal number of earned points when buying a premium product instead of a standard product, and the relative weight w of incorporating these, normatively irrelevant, nominal differences in the number of credited points into purchase decisions.

The following sections report findings from three studies. Similar to the above study series, the first investigation (study 7) serves as an initial test of the proposed effect of medium magnitude on purchase decisions by analyzing how scheme members' product choices depend on the magnitude of a loyalty program currency. Thus, keeping the outcome/input ratios of the available standard and premium products constant, this study isolates the effect of the nominal differences in the number of earned points when buying a premium product instead of a standard product. In a next step, study 8 addresses the hypothesized moderating effect of dominance between choice options in the purchase decision context. Hence, this survey explores situations where the medium magnitude effect disappears or—to put it more formally—circumstances where the relative weight w of incorporating medium magnitude into decision-making descends steeply. Finally, study 9 aims to confirm the external validity of the medium magnitude effect on purchase decisions by means of a heterogeneous sample structure.

3.1 Study 7

3.1.1 Participants, Design, and Procedure

For an initial test of hypothesis 3a, 79 students (M_{age}= 24.7 years, 59.5% female) were recruited to take part in a single-factor, between-subjects study with two conditions (low versus high medium magnitude). Using the railway company cover story, participants were asked to imagine that they frequently traveled by train to visit a friend living 300 kilometers away and that they were participating in a loyalty program of the fictive railway company they regularly used for their trips. Participants then were told that they were planning a journey for the next weekend and were confronted with the choice between a standard ticket (travel time 3h 12m, economy train) and a premium ticket (travel time 2h 50m, comfort express train). The price of the standard ticket was indicated with €40, whereas the premium ticket was priced at €50. Medium magnitude was manipulated such that members in the high (low) medium magnitude condition earned 100 points (1 point) per €10 spent on the railway company (see figure 18). In both conditions the proposed program reward was a standard ticket that required—depending on the medium magnitude condition—40 and 4,000 points, respectively.

Figure 18. Travel Options of Study 7

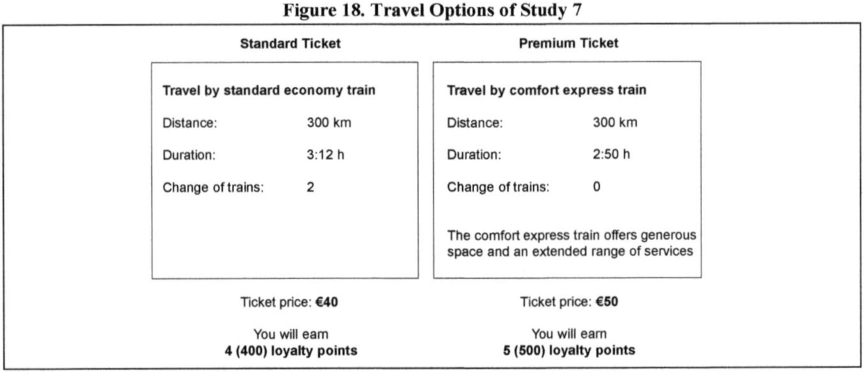

Subsequent to the choice between the premium and the standard ticket, subjects were asked to indicate their perceptions of the magnitude of the presented program medium (Bagchi and Lee 2011) in order to evaluate the manipulation's performance. To check for potential differences between respondents in different experimental conditions, price consciousness

($\alpha = .77$, factor loadings $\geq .77$; Donthu and Garcia 1999) and quality consciousness ($\alpha = .75$, factor loadings $\geq .76$; Ailawadi et al. 2001) were assessed on seven-point scales, anchored by "strongly disagree" (1) and "strongly agree" (7). In addition, to capture participants' attitude toward loyalty programs the number of loyalty cards permanently in the wallet was also measured.

3.1.2 Results

3.1.2.1 Manipulation Check and Control Variables

Respondents' ratings of the perceived number of credited points confirmed that the manipulation of medium magnitude worked as intended. Specifically, respondents in the high magnitude condition evaluated the number of points earned per euro spent significantly higher ($M_{\text{mm-high}} = 4.65$) than participants in the low magnitude condition ($M_{\text{mm-low}} = 2.19$, $t(77) = 11.62$, $p < .01$). Furthermore, neither the number of loyalty program memberships ($M_{\text{mm-low}} = 2.29$ versus $M_{\text{mm-high}} = 2.56$, $t(77) = .63$, n.s.), nor price consciousness ($M_{\text{mm-low}} = 5.06$ versus $M_{\text{mm-high}} = 4.85$, $t(77) = .68$, n.s.), or quality consciousness ($M_{\text{mm-low}} = 4.17$ versus $M_{\text{mm-highest}} = 4.02$, $t(77) = .55$, n.s.) significantly differed between both experimental groups; precluding that different choice shares between the high and the low magnitude condition have to be ascribed to respondents' attitudes.

2.1.2.2 Hypothesis

The results of this study are summarized in figure 19. Of the 39 respondents in the high magnitude condition, 56.4 percent (22 respondents) preferred the premium ticket over the standard ticket (43.6%, 17 respondents). In contrast, of the 40 participants who were confronted with the low magnitude program, only 32.5 percent (13 respondents) chose the premium ticket instead of the standard ticket (67.5%, 27 respondents). Thus, as predicted in hypothesis 3a, subjects who encountered the high magnitude program were significantly more likely to buy the premium ticket ($\chi^2(1) = 4.58$, $p < .05$); providing a first confirmation of the proposed medium magnitude effect on purchase decisions.

Figure 19. The Effect of Medium Magnitude on the Choice between Premium and Standard Products

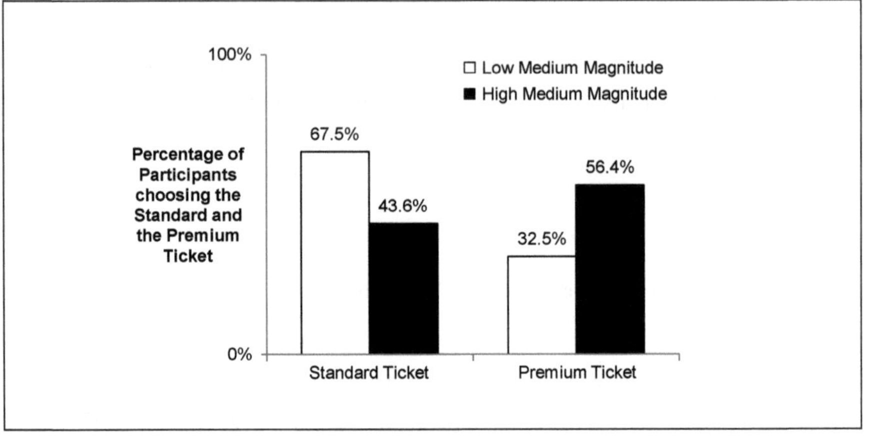

3.2 Study 8

3.2.1 Participants, Design, and Procedure

After study 7 has demonstrated that the magnitude of a program medium influences scheme members' purchase decisions according to the predicted manner (H3a), the purpose of study 8 is to additionally confirm this finding in a different context and to analyze the proposed moderating effect of dominance between choice options (H4a). Therefore, Study 8 was designed as a 2 (low versus high medium magnitude) × 2 (low versus high dominance between choice options) full-factorial, between-subjects experiment. Students who registered online for marketing classes at TU Dortmund University were invited via e-mail to take part in this online study. One hundred seventy-nine respondents (M_{age} = 21.9 years, 64.8% female) completed the questionnaire and answered control questions correctly. Cell sizes ranged from n = 42 to n = 47.

The study scenarios asked participants to imagine that they were participating in a loyalty program of the supermarket they visited most frequently. This program's reward was a €10 voucher which required an accumulative spending of €100. Moreover, participants were told that they were shopping for groceries and were confronted with the choice between two shopping baskets; the first basket solely consisted of private label products (standard basket, A), whereas the second basket merely contained branded products (premium basket, B).

3.2.2 Operationalization of Variables

3.2.2.1 Independent Variables

In accordance with the above studies, medium magnitude was varied such that the number of points earned in high magnitude program represents a multiple of the monetary amount spent on the company, whereas the number of points earned in the low magnitude program constitutes a fraction of the amount spent. Specifically, participants assigned to one of the low magnitude conditions earned 1 point per €5 spent on groceries, while respondents encountered the high magnitude programs were credited 10 points for every €5 spent. Consequently, the €10 voucher reward required the accumulation of 20 points in the low and 200 points in the high magnitude groups, respectively.

The dominance between choice options—i.e. between the standard basket and the premium basket—was manipulated by varying the price of the premium basket and, thus, its outcome/input ratio. As can be seen in figure 20, keeping the standard basket's price constant at €10, the price of the premium basket increased from €15 in the low dominance condition to €20 in the high dominance condition.

Figure 20. Shopping Baskets of Study 8

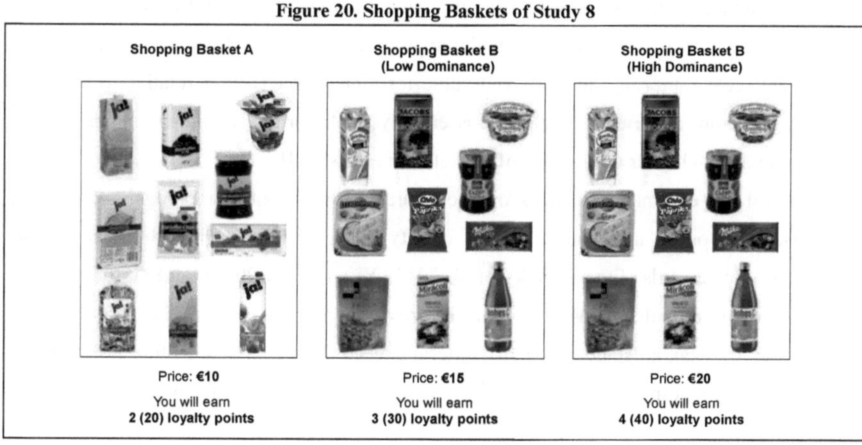

Regarding the low dominance treatment, the choice between basket A and basket B might involve a choice conflict. Whereas basket A is better on the price dimension, basket B is expected to be perceived as superior regarding quality. Hence, analysis of dominance structures between the available choice options might not procure sufficient reasons for choice. In this case—similar to study 7—it is expected that medium magnitude enhances the likelihood of choosing the premium basket. Conversely, the fact that the standard basket in the high dominance conditions costs half as much as the premium basket might overcompensate its disadvantage on the quality dimension such that an analysis of dominance structures should be in favor of the standard basket. In this case, there may be a coherent argument for the choice among both shopping baskets which is assumed to reduce the impact of medium magnitude.

3.2.2.2 Dependent Variable, Manipulation Checks, and Covariates

After processing the cover story and the choice problem, participants provided their preferences regarding the two presented shopping baskets on a seven-point scale anchored by "1 = strongly prefer shopping basket A and 7 = strongly prefer shopping basket B" (e.g., Barone and Roy 2010; Gourville and Soman 1998). Thus, higher (lower) numbers on this measure reflect a stronger preference for the premium (standard) basket.

The impact of the manipulations of medium magnitude and dominance between choice options was gauged via responses to manipulation check questions. The performance of the magnitude manipulation was assessed using the same manipulation check item as in the above studies (Bagchi and Li 2011). To evaluate the appropriateness of the dominance manipulation a multi-item scale capturing the perceived value for money of basket A relative to basket B (Hardesty, Carlson, and Bearden 2002) was employed. Accordingly, higher ratings on this measure represent a higher dominance of basket A over basket B.

To control for external influences on the choice between both shopping baskets price consciousness (Donthu and Garcia 1999), quality consciousness (Ailawadi et al. 2001), attractiveness of rewards (Evanschitzky et al. 2011; Yi and Jeon 2003), and attitude toward loyalty programs were also measured. Table 19 provides an overview of all items used in this study. As can be seen, all standard quality criteria exceed the recommended thresholds. Thus, for further analysis, responses to multiple item scales were averaged to form a single score for each construct.

Table 19. Operationalization of Latent Variables (Study 8)

Latent Variables and Items	Factor Loadings
Dependent Variable	
Likelihood of Buying a Premium Basket over a Standard Basket	
▪ Which of the two shopping baskets would you prefer to buy? ("1 = strongly prefer shopping basket A" to "7 = strongly prefer shopping basket B")	-
Manipulation Checks	
Medium Magnitude	
▪ This program offers a large number of points per euro spent.	-
Dominance Between Choice Options (α = .78)	
When compared to basket B ...	
▪ ... basket A is a very good value for money	.87
▪ ... basket A is worth the money	.88
▪ ... basket A is a very good buy for the money	.76
Control Variables	
Perceived Attractiveness of Rewards (ρ = .76; r = .62, p < .01)	
▪ The proposed rewards have high cash value.	.90
▪ The proposed rewards are what I want.	.90
Price Consciousness (α = . 77)	
▪ When shopping, I often find myself checking the prices.	.73
▪ One can save a lot of money by shopping around for bargains.	.86
▪ I usually purchase items on sale only.	.89
Quality Consciousness (α = .77)	
▪ I will not give up high quality for a lower price.	.75
▪ I always buy the best.	.88
▪ It is important to me to buy high-quality products.	.86
Attitude toward Loyalty Programs	
▪ How many loyalty cards do you have permanently in your wallet?	-

Note: All measures not indicated otherwise were assessed on seven-point scales anchored by "strongly disagree" (1) and "strongly agree" (7).

3.2.3 Results

3.2.3.1 Manipulation Checks

An ANOVA with the perceived number of points earned per euro spent elicited only a main effect of the magnitude of the program medium ($F(1, 175) = 6.57, p < .05$). Consistent with the magnitude manipulation, respondents in the high magnitude conditions on average rated the perceived number of earned points as higher ($M_{\text{mm-high}} = 4.43$) compared to those who were exposed to a low magnitude program ($M_{\text{mm-low}} = 3.78$, $t(177) = 2.59$, $p < .05$). Moreover, an ANOVA with the perceived value for money of basket A relative to basket B elicited a significant main effect of the dominance manipulation ($F(1, 175) = 4.36$, $p < .05$); confirming that perceived dominance of basket A over basket B significantly increased with the €5 price increase of basket B ($M_{\text{dom-low}} = 4.56$ versus $M_{\text{dom-high}} = 4.97$, $t(177) = 2.15$, $p < .05$). Since no other effects emerged, both manipulations worked as intended.

3.2.3.2 Hypotheses

An ANCOVA with the perceived attractiveness of rewards ($F(1, 171) = .01$, n.s.), price consciousness ($F(1, 171) = 26.53, p < .01$), quality consciousness ($F(1, 171) = 29.20, p < .01$), and attitude toward loyalty programs ($F(1, 171) = 1.37$, n.s.) used as covariates revealed a significant main effect of dominance between choice options ($F(1, 171) = 12.12, p < .01$) and a significant dominance × medium magnitude interaction ($F(1, 171) = 4.46$, $p < .05$) on the likelihood of buying the premium basket. Contrary to expectations, the main effect of the magnitude of the program medium ($F(1, 171) = 2.18$, n.s.) cannot be supported. These results are summarized in table 20.

An examination of the directions of the observed effects revealed that an increased dominance of basket A over basket B significantly diminished the likelihood of buying the premium basket B ($M_{\text{dom-low}} = 3.57$ versus $M_{\text{dom-high}} = 2.56$, $t(177) =3.49$, $p < .01$). In addition, although the main effect of medium magnitude could not be supported, analysis of the significant interaction effect showed that—in line with H4a—medium magnitude still had a positive impact on the likelihood of choosing the premium basket in case of low dominance ($M_{\text{mm-low}} = 2.86$ versus $M_{\text{mm-high}} = 4.21$, $t(87) = 3.07$, $p < .01$) which was not present when comparing both high dominance groups ($M_{\text{mm-low}} = 2.76$ versus $M_{\text{mm-high}} = 2.36$, $t(88) = 1.12$, n.s). These effects remain unchanged when controlling for attractiveness of rewards, price consciousness, quality consciousness, and attitude toward loyalty programs ($F_{dom\text{-}low}(1, 83) = 4.11$, $p < .05$ and $F_{dom\text{-}high}(1, 84) = .47$, n.s.). Hence, similar to consumer choices in the participation and redemption decision context, a discernable dominance structure between choice options is able to attenuate the medium magnitude effect on purchase decisions. These results are summarized in figure 21.

Table 20. ANCOVA Results of Study 8

	F	*p*
Main Effects		
Medium Magnitude	2.18	n.s.
Dominance Between Choice Options	12.12	< .01
Interaction Effect		
Medium Magnitude × Dominance Between Choice Options	4.46	< .05
Covariates		
Perceived Attractiveness of Rewards	.01	n.s.
Price Consciousness	26.53	< .01
Quality Consciousness	29.20	< .01
Attitude toward Loyalty Programs	1.37	n.s.

Figure 21. The Effect of Medium Magnitude and Dominance between Choice Options on the Likelihood of Buying a Premium Basket over a Standard Basket

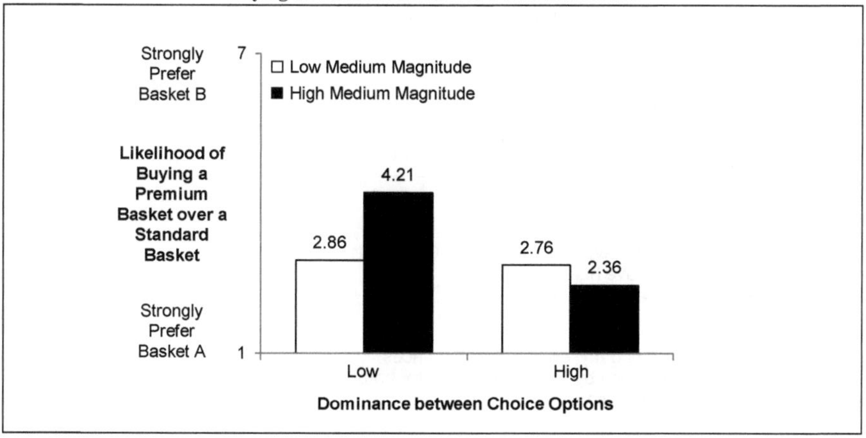

3.3 Study 9

3.3.1 Participants, Design, and Procedure

Finally, to provide an evaluation of the external validity of the acquired findings regarding the medium magnitude effect on purchase decisions, the last investigation in this choice context, study 9, was an exact replicate of study 8 with the exception that a heterogeneous sample structure was accessed. Two hundred and twenty-seven participants (M_{age} = 33.8 years, SD_{age} = 13.53, 68.3% female) were recruited via social media platforms and available email addresses. The majority of respondents was either employed or self-employed (61.6%; 23.8% students, and 14.5% retired, house-maker, or jobless). Table 21 provides an overview of the used measurement models which—consistent with study 8—exhibit a satisfactory level of internal consistency.

Table 21. Operationalization of Latent Variables (Study 9)

Latent Variables and Items	Factor Loadings
Dependent Variable	
Likelihood of Buying a Premium Basket over a Standard Basket	
▪ Which of the two shopping baskets would you prefer to buy? ("strongly prefer shopping basket A" to "strongly prefer shopping basket B")	-
Manipulation Checks	
Medium Magnitude	
▪ This program offers a large number of points per euro spent.	-
Dominance Between Choice Options (α = .82)	
When compared to basket B ...	
▪ ... basket A is a very good value for money	.87
▪ ... basket A is worth the money	.92
▪ ... basket A is a very good buy for the money	.72
Control Variables	
Perceived Attractiveness of Rewards (ρ = . 81; r = .67, p < .01)	
▪ The proposed rewards have high cash value.	.92
▪ The proposed rewards are what I want.	.92
Price Consciousness (α = . 80)	
▪ When shopping, I often find myself checking the prices.	.82
▪ One can save a lot of money by shopping around for bargains.	.81
▪ I usually purchase items on sale only.	.91

Table 21. (continued)

Latent Variables and Items	Factor Loadings
Quality Consciousness (α = .77)	
▪ I will not give up high quality for a lower price.	.72
▪ I always buy the best.	.89
▪ It is important to me to buy high-quality products.	.89
Attitude toward Loyalty Programs	
▪ How many loyalty cards do you have permanently in your wallet?	-

Note: All measures not indicated otherwise were assessed on seven-point scales anchored by "strongly disagree" (1) and "strongly agree" (7).

3.3.2 Results

3.3.2.1 Manipulation Checks

Respondents' ratings of the perception of medium magnitude confirmed that the manipulation of this independent variable worked as intended. Specifically, an ANOVA with points earned per euro spent elicited only a significant main effect of program magnitude ($F(1, 223) = 28.06$, $p < .01$). Participants in the high magnitude conditions were aware that they were earning a higher number of points per euro spent relative to those in the low magnitude conditions ($M_{\text{mm-low}} = 3.46$ versus $M_{\text{mm-high}} = 4.79$, $t(225) = 5.31$, $p < .01$). In addition, an ANOVA with the perceived value for money of basket A relative to basket B revealed a significant main effect of the dominance manipulation ($F(1, 223) = 32.81$, $p < .01$), such that increasing the price of the premium basket significantly enhanced the perceived dominance of the standard basket over the premium basket ($M_{\text{dom-low}} = 4.18$ versus $M_{\text{dom-high}} = 5.33$, $t(225) = 5.77$, $p < .01$). No other effects emerged; suggesting that this manipulation worked as expected as well.

3.3.2.2 Hypotheses

An ANCOVA with the perceived attractiveness of rewards ($F(1, 219) = .00$, n.s.), price consciousness ($F(1, 219) = 27.08$, $p < .01$), quality consciousness ($F(1, 219) = 22.84$, $p < .01$), and attitude toward loyalty programs ($F(1, 219) = 1.00$, n.s.) used as covariates revealed significant main effects of medium magnitude ($F(1, 219) = 4.72$, $p < .05$) and dominance between choice options ($F(1, 219) = 6.51$, $p < .05$) on the likelihood of buying the premium basket. However, unlike study 8, the dominance × medium magnitude interaction ($F(1, 219) = 1.37$, n.s.) cannot be supported. These results are summarized in table 22.

Table 22. ANCOVA Results of Study 9

	F	*p*
Main Effects		
Medium Magnitude	4.72	< .05
Dominance Between Choice Options	6.51	< .05
Interaction Effect		
Medium Magnitude × Dominance Between Choice Options	1.37	n.s.
Covariates		
Perceived Attractiveness of Rewards	.00	n.s.
Price Consciousness	27.08	< .01
Quality Consciousness	22.84	< .01
Attitude toward Loyalty Programs	1.00	n.s.

A closer look at these effects confirmed that an increased dominance of basket A over basket B significantly reduced the likelihood of buying the premium basket B ($M_{\text{dom-low}} = 3.34$ versus $M_{\text{dom-high}} = 2.53$, $t(255) = 2.91$, $p < .01$). In addition, as proposed in hypothesis 3a, medium magnitude had a positive effect on the likelihood of buying the premium basket ($M_{\text{mm-low}} = 2.56$ versus $M_{\text{mm-high}} = 3.27$, $t(255) = 2.54$, $p < .05$). Moreover, although the interaction effect was not significant, further analyses of simple contrasts affirmed that the preference for the premium basket was only affected by medium magnitude when dominance was low ($M_{\text{mm-low}} = 2.84$ versus $M_{\text{mm-high}} = 3.81$, $t(111) = 2.29$, $p < .05$) and not in case of high dominance ($M_{\text{mm-low}} = 2.29$ versus $M_{\text{mm-high}} = 2.75$, $t(112) = 1.30$, n.s.). These effects remain unchanged when controlling for attractiveness of rewards, price consciousness, quality consciousness, and attitude toward loyalty programs ($F_{\text{dom-low}}(1, 107) = 4.96$, $p < .05$ and $F_{\text{dom-high}}(1, 108) = .50$, n.s.). Thus, consistent with study 8 and in line with hypothesis 4a, dominance between choice options constitutes a boundary condition of medium magnitude effect in the purchase decision context. Figure 22 illustrates this finding.

Figure 22. The Effect of Medium Magnitude and Dominance between Choice Options on the Likelihood of Buying a Premium Basket over a Standard Basket

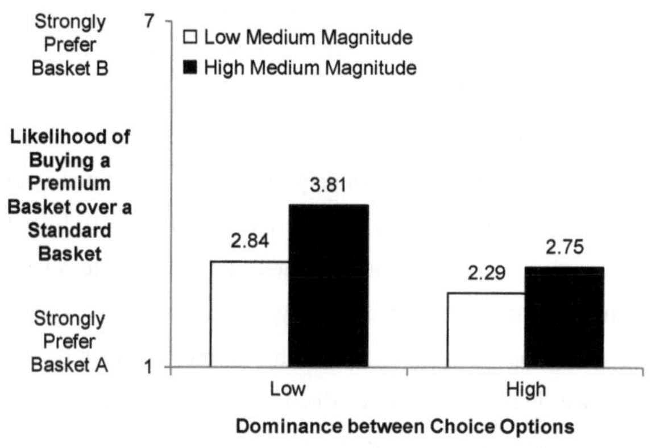

3.4 Discussion

The study series in this chapter sheds light on the proposed medium magnitude effect on the choice between products of different quality and prices. The presented investigations suggest that loyalty program members—when choosing between premium and standard products—do not merely focus their attention to differences in outcome/input ratios of the available choice options but also take differences in the nominal number of earned points into account.

Specifically, as posited in hypothesis 3a, study 7 affirms that the magnitude of a loyalty program medium affects scheme members' purchase decisions in the predicted manner. In this experiment, the loyalty programs under consideration solely differed regarding their level of medium magnitude and, thus, varied among the number of additional credited points when buying a premium product instead of a standard product. However, since the rewards of both programs required exactly the same effort—i.e. the same monetary amount spent on the company—to redeem a reward, these differences should not influence choice and, consequently, product preferences between members of the low and members of the high magnitude program should be equivalent. Nonetheless, this study supports the assumption that individuals overvalue the nominal differences in the number of credited points—formally, $m_{pp}^{low/high} - m_{sp}^{low/high}$—such that people are more likely to buy a premium product instead of a standard product when they were participating in a high magnitude program than when they were enrolled in a low magnitude program. In other words, a high magnitude of a program currency seems to make scheme members less price sensitive.

In addition to supporting the medium magnitude effect on purchase decisions in a different context, study 8 also confirms the proposed boundary condition. As posited in hypothesis 4a, when dominance between the choice options is high, individuals merely base their product decisions on an assessment of the outcome/input ratios of the available alternatives which degrades the effect of medium magnitude. Conversely, when dominance structures between choice options do not provide appropriate reasons for choice, program members become prone to use the nominal differences in the number of credited points when buying a premium product instead of a standard product inappropriately to make inferences about the attractiveness of the choice options under consideration and, thus, the medium magnitude effect occurs.

Finally, study 9 demonstrates the robustness of the phenomenon that purchase intentions of more expensive premium products increase due to a high medium magnitude and its boundary condition by replicating the findings from study 8 with a heterogeneous sample structure.

4 The Impact of Medium Magnitude on Reward Decisions

This chapter concentrates on the medium magnitude effect in the last identified decision context; namely, program members' choice between different rewards. Precisely, the following studies investigate the hypothesized negative impact of medium magnitude on the likelihood of redeeming a premium reward instead of a standard reward (H3b) and the moderating effect of dominance between choice options in the reward decision context (H4b). Formally, the subsequent examinations are centered toward the elements of equation 19,

$$L_{\text{redeem}}^{\text{low/high}}(\text{pr; pr, sr}) = (1 - \text{w}) \cdot \text{v}\left(\frac{\text{Outcome}_{\text{pr}}}{\text{Input}_{\text{pr}}} - \frac{\text{Outcome}_{\text{sr}}}{\text{Input}_{\text{sr}}}\right) + \text{w} \cdot \text{v}\left(-\left|\text{m}_{\text{pr}}^{\text{low/high}} - \text{m}_{\text{sr}}^{\text{low/high}}\right|\right), \quad (19)$$

which posits that the likelihood of redeeming a premium reward pr over a standard reward sr depends on the perceived difference in the outcome/input ratio of the premium and the standard reward under consideration, the perceived difference in the nominal number of loyalty points required to redeem a premium reward instead of a standard reward, and the relative weight w which reflects the degree to which this nominal difference in the number of requisite points is incorporated into reward decisions. Note that, variations in the number of extra points required to redeem a premium reward instead of a standard reward are solely affected by the magnitude of the program currency and do not influence the requirements to obtain a premium reward in real terms.

The proposed medium magnitude effect on reward decisions was tested in three studies. The following studies 10 and 11 investigate experimentally how loyalty program members' reward preferences are influenced by the magnitude of a loyalty program currency. More specifically, study 10 examines this effect in isolation by merely varying the program's medium magnitude and, consequently, the nominal price differences between premium and standard rewards while keeping the outcome/input ratios of the rewards under consideration constant. In a next step, study 11 provides insights regarding relative weight parameter by placing the prediction that dominance structures between the available rewards are able to alleviate this effect under scrutiny. Finally, study 12 aims to confirm the external validity of the medium magnitude effect on reward choices based on the already presented customer survey about loyalty program members' perceptions of and behavior in existing real-world loyalty schemes (see study 6).

4.1 Study 10

4.1.1 Participants, Design, and Procedure

For an initial test of hypothesis 3b a single-factor, between-subjects online experiment with two conditions (low versus high medium magnitude) was conducted. Responses of 87 students (M_{age} = 23.5 years, 49.4% female) who completed the questionnaire and answered control questions consistently regarding to the provided scenario texts were used for analysis.

Using the railway company cover story, the study scenarios asked participants to imagine that they frequently traveled by train to visit a friend living 300 kilometers away and that they were participating in a loyalty program of the fictive railway company they regularly used for their trips. Subjects then were told that they already accumulated enough points to redeem a single ticket for their next trip and were confronted with the choice between a standard ticket, a premium ticket, and non-redemption. Besides information about the number of points required for each travel reward, information about the requisite number of collected points for round-trip tickets—that was not yet reached—was provided, such that the no-choice option was also plausible. Figure 23 illustrates the programs' travel rewards and their prices.

Figure 23. Travel Rewards of Study 10

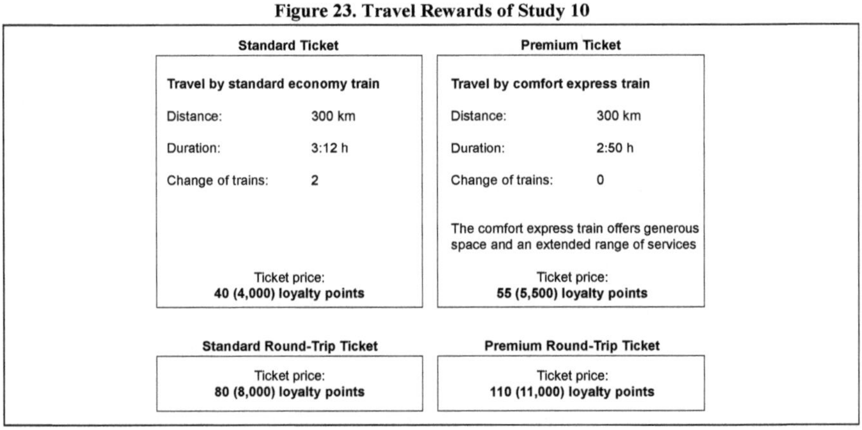

The magnitude of the loyalty program currency was manipulated, such that respondents in the high (low) medium magnitude condition were told that the loyalty program credits its members 100 loyalty points (1 loyalty point) per €10 spent on the company and that they accrued 6,000 (60) points through their last journeys. The single standard ticket reward was priced at 4,000 (40) points, whereas the premium ticket price was indicated with 5,500 (55) points (see figure 23). To assess the performance of the manipulation of medium magnitude, participants were asked to indicate their perception of the number of points required to redeem a reward on a seven-point scale. To check for potential differences between respondents in the high and low medium magnitude groups, price consciousness ($\alpha = .77$, Donthu and Garcia 1999), perceived attractiveness of rewards ($\rho = .65$; $r = .48$, $p < .01$; Evanschitzky et al. 2011; Yi and Jeon 2003), and attitude toward loyalty programs—i.e. the number of loyalty cards permanently in the wallet—were measured.

4.1.2 Results

4.1.2.1 Manipulation Check and Control Variables

Respondents' ratings of the perception of the number of points required for redemption confirmed that the manipulation of medium magnitude worked as intended. Specifically, participants in the low magnitude conditions perceived the number of requisite points significantly lower ($M_{\text{mm-low}} = 4.07$) than those who encountered the high magnitude program ($M_{\text{mm-high}} = 4.79$, $t(85) = 2.28$, $p < .05$). Moreover, neither price consciousness ($M_{\text{mm-low}} = 4.91$ versus $M_{\text{mm-high}} = 4.96$, $t(85) = .20$, n.s.), nor perceived attractiveness of rewards ($M_{\text{mm-low}} = .85$ versus $M_{\text{mm-high}} = 4.06$, $t(85) = .74$, n.s.), nor the number of loyalty cards permanently in the wallet ($M_{\text{mm-low}} = 2.11$ versus $M_{\text{mm-high}} = 1.86$, $t(85) = .64$, n.s.) significantly differed between experimental groups; precluding that differences in reward choice shares have to be ascribed to these variables.

4.1.2.2 Hypotheses

Before testing hypothesis 3b, the collected data was used to provide additional support for hypothesis 1b which assumes a negative effect of medium magnitude on the general likelihood to redeem accumulated points. Therefore, in a first step, participants' choice between redemption—irrespective of the reward chosen—and non-redemption was examined. As shown in figure 24, more participants preferred redemption (75.6%, 34 of 45 respondents) over non-redemption (24.4%, 11 respondents) in the low medium magnitude condition than in the high medium magnitude condition, where only 54.8 percent (23 of 42 respondents) chose to redeem one of the both offered rewards. A χ^2-test revealed that these differences in choice shares were statistically significant ($\chi^2(1) = 4.16, p < .05$). This result is in line with hypothesis 1b and, thus, provides further evidence for the negative effect of medium magnitude on redemption behavior.

Figure 24. The Effect of Medium Magnitude on the Choice between Redemption and Non-Redemption

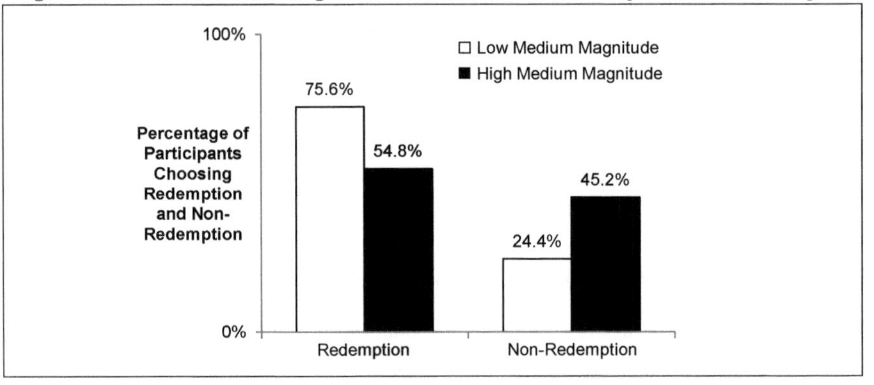

Considering the choice between the premium and the standard ticket rewards, further analysis of the subjects who decided to redeem their accumulated points revealed a significant difference in the choice shares among rewards ($\chi^2(1) = 4.31, p < .05$) between the low and the high magnitude condition (see figure 25).

Figure 25. The Effect of Medium Magnitude on the Choice between Premium and Standard Rewards

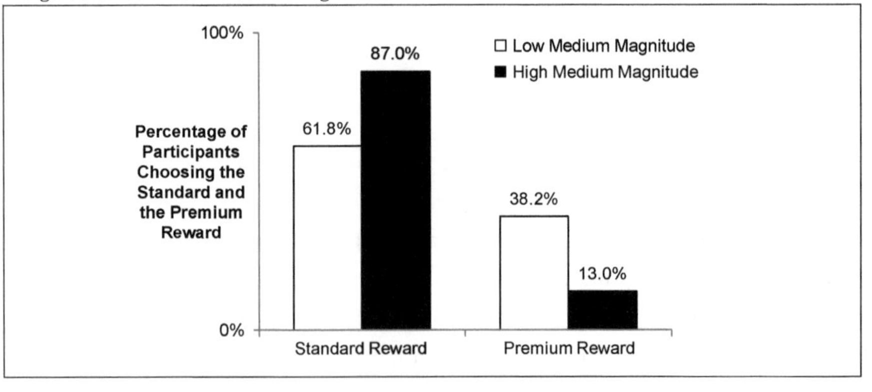

Consistent with hypothesis 3b, significantly more respondents chose to redeem a premium ticket (38.2%, 13 of 34 respondents) over a standard ticket (61.8%, 21 respondents) when they were exposed to the low magnitude program than those who encountered the high magnitude scheme (13.0%, 3 of 23 respondents).

4.2 Study 11

4.2.1 Participants, Design, and Procedure

Subsequent to the initial demonstration of the negative effect of medium magnitude on the likelihood of redeeming a premium reward over a standard reward provided by study 10, study 11 sheds light on the proposed boundary condition of this effect. More specifically, aside from confirming the identified negative impact of the magnitude of a loyalty program medium on premium reward preferences, this study investigates the assumed moderating effect of dominance between choice options (H4b). To this end, marketing students at TU Dortmund University were asked via email to take part in an online study. One hundred ninety-six respondents (M_{age} = 22.0 years, 64.8% female) completed the questionnaire and answered control questions correctly. Study 11 was designed as a 2 (low versus high medium magnitude) × 2 (low versus high dominance between choice options) full-factorial, between-subjects experiment. Participants were randomly assigned to one of the four resulting experimental conditions. Cell sizes ranged from $n = 48$ to $n = 50$.

Using the same cover story as in study 10, the study scenarios indicated that participants had enrolled in a railway company's loyalty program because they frequently traveled by train to visit a friend. Participants then were told that they had already collected enough points to redeem a single ticket for their next trip and were confronted with the choice between a standard ticket and a premium ticket. Hence, the choice problem had a similar format as study 10. However, unlike the above study, subjects were told to imagine that they had decided to redeem a free ticket, such that non-redemption was not an option. Thus, participants were merely asked to indicate their preferences between the standard and the premium travel reward.

4.2.2 Operationalization of Variables

4.2.2.1 Independent Variables

In accordance with study 10, program members in the high (low) medium magnitude conditions earned 100 points (1 point) per €10 spent on the company. In addition, participants were informed that they accumulated 7,200 (72) points with their last journeys. Thus, irrespective of the magnitude of the program currency, participants in all experimental conditions had already spent €720 on the railway company.

The dominance structure between choice options—i.e. dominance between the standard and the premium reward—was manipulated by varying the number of requisite points to redeem the premium ticket and, thus, the outcome/input ratio of the premium ticket. All participants learned that the standard ticket was priced at—depending on the specification of medium magnitude—40 or 4,000 points, respectively. Similar to study 10, in the low dominance conditions, the premium ticket could be redeem for 55 (5,500) points. In contrast, the price of the premium ticket in the high dominance conditions was indicated with 70 (7,000) points. Figure 26 illustrates the resulting travel reward prices depending on the presented program's medium magnitude and dominance manipulation.

Figure 26. Travel Rewards of Study 11

Standard Ticket	Premium Ticket (Low Dominance)	Premium Ticket (High Dominance)
Travel by standard economy train	**Travel by comfort express train**	**Travel by comfort express train**
Distance: 300 km	Distance: 300 km	Distance: 300 km
Duration: 3:12 h	Duration: 2:50 h	Duration: 2:50 h
Change of trains: 2	Change of trains: 0	Change of trains: 0
	The comfort express train offers generous space and an extended range of services	The comfort express train offers generous space and an extended range of services
Price: **40 (4,000) loyalty points**	Price: **55 (5,500) loyalty points**	Price: **70 (7,000) loyalty points**

In the low dominance conditions, the choice between the premium and the standard ticket might not be trivial. Whereas the standard ticket requires program members to abandon fewer points than the premium ticket, the premium reward might be perceived as superior with regards to quality. Given this expected choice conflict, examination of dominance structures might not provide a solid basis for the choice between both rewards. In this case, in accordance with study 10, it is expected that the negative medium magnitude effect on the likelihood of choosing the premium reward occurs. However, increasing the number of points needed to redeem the premium ticket should yield an explicit dominance of the standard over the premium travel reward, such that the reward choices become less sensitive toward variations of the specification of medium magnitude.

4.2.2.2 Dependent Variable, Manipulation Checks, and Covariates

Subsequent to the introduction of the choice problem, participants were asked to indicate their preferences between the two presented travel rewards on a seven-point scale anchored by "1 = strongly prefer the standard ticket" and "7 = strongly prefer the premium ticket" (e.g., Barone and Roy 2010; Gourville and Soman 1998). Thus, higher (lower) values on this measure indicate a stronger preference for the premium (standard) reward.

The appropriateness of the developed manipulations was assessed by means of participants' responses to manipulation-check questions. In accordance with study 10, the perception of medium magnitude was evaluated with the statement "This program requires a large number of points to redeem a reward", whereas dominance between choice options was measured with the perceived value for price of the standard ticket relative to premium ticket (Hardesty et al. 2002). To control for potential external influences on the preference between the standard and the premium reward, participants evaluated several covariate measures; price consciousness (Donthu and Garcia 1999), quality consciousness (Ailawadi et al. 2001), attractiveness of rewards (Evanschitzky et al. 2011; Yi and Jeon 2003), and attitude toward loyalty programs were assessed using the scales of the above studies. Table 23 shows that the assessment of quality criteria of all multi-item scales affirms apt measurement models of the latent variables. For further analysis, simple averages were calculated from the raw scores of responses to multiple items of the same construct.

Table 23. Operationalization of Latent Variables (Study 11)

Latent Variables and Items	Factor Loadings
Dependent Variable	
Likelihood of Redeeming a Premium Reward over a Standard Reward	
▪ Which of the two rewards would you prefer to redeem? ("strongly prefer the standard ticket" to "strongly prefer the premium ticket")	-
Manipulation Checks	
Medium Magnitude	
▪ This program requires a large number of points to redeem a reward.	-
Dominance Between Choice Options (α = .80) When compared to premium ticket ...	
▪ ... the standard ticket is a very good value for its price	.83
▪ ... the standard ticket is worth its price	.88
▪ ... the standard ticket is a very good choice	.82
Control Variables	
Perceived Attractiveness of Rewards (ρ = .59; r = .42, p < .01)	
▪ The proposed rewards have high cash value.	.84
▪ The proposed rewards are what I want.	.84
Price Consciousness (α = . 81)	
▪ When shopping, I often find myself checking the prices.	.80
▪ One can save a lot of money by shopping around for bargains.	.88
▪ I usually purchase items on sale only.	.87
Quality Consciousness (α = .77)	
▪ I will not give up high quality for a lower price.	.70
▪ I always buy the best.	.90
▪ It is important to me to buy high-quality products.	.89
Attitude toward Loyalty Programs	
▪ How many loyalty cards do you have permanently in your wallet?	-

Note: All measures not indicated otherwise were assessed on seven-point scales anchored by "strongly disagree" (1) and "strongly agree" (7).

4.2.3 Results

4.2.3.1 Manipulation Checks

An ANOVA with perceptions of the number of points required for redemption revealed only a significant main effect of the manipulation of medium magnitude ($F(1, 192) = 8.45, p < .01$). Since subjects in the high magnitude treatment conditions perceived the amount of requisite points significantly higher ($M_{\text{mm-high}} = 4.76$) than those in the low magnitude groups ($M_{\text{mm-low}} = 4.08$, $t(194) = 2.92, p < .01$), this manipulation worked in the expected direction. In addition, an ANOVA with perceived value for price of the standard ticket relative to the premium ticket elicited a significant main effect of the dominance manipulation ($F(1, 192) = 25.45, p < .01$), such that the perceived value for price of the standard ticket significantly ascended with an increased number of points required to redeem a premium ticket ($M_{\text{dom-low}} = 3.38$ versus $M_{\text{dom-high}} = 4.32$, $t(194) = 5.05, p < .01$). No other effects emerged; suggesting that the manipulation of dominance between choice options worked as intended.

4.2.3.2 Hypotheses

An ANCOVA with the perceived attractiveness of rewards ($F(1, 188) = .23$, n.s.), price consciousness ($F(1, 188) = .00$, n.s.), quality consciousness ($F(1, 188) = 10.33, p < .01$), and attitude toward loyalty programs ($F(1, 188) = 2.42$, n.s.) used as covariates revealed significant main effects of medium magnitude ($F(1, 188) = 9.16, p < .01$) and dominance between choice options ($F(1, 188) = 6.24, p < .05$) on the likelihood of redeeming the premium ticket. Moreover, a significant dominance × medium magnitude interaction ($F(1, 188) = 3.23, p < .10$) emerged. These results are summarized in table 24.

As proposed in hypothesis 3b, medium magnitude had a negative effect on the likelihood of redeeming a premium reward over a standard reward, as indicated by a significant stronger preference for the premium ticket in the low magnitude conditions ($M_{\text{mm-low}} = 3.88$) than in the high magnitude conditions ($M_{\text{mm-high}} = 2.97$, $t(194) = 2.82, p < .01$). In addition, an increasing dominance of the standard ticket over the premium ticket decreased the likelihood of redeeming the premium ticket ($M_{\text{dom-low}} = 3.87$ versus $M_{\text{dom-high}} = 2.96$, $t(194) = 2.84, p < .01$).

Table 24. ANCOVA Results of Study 11

	F	*p*
Main Effects		
Medium Magnitude	9.16	< .01
Dominance between Choice Options	6.24	< .05
Interaction Effect		
Medium Magnitude × Dominance Between Choice Options	3.23	< .10
Covariates		
Perceived Attractiveness of Rewards	.23	n.s.
Price Consciousness	.00	n.s.
Quality Consciousness	10.33	< .01
Attitude toward Loyalty Programs	2.42	n.s.

The test of hypothesis 4b requires the comparison of two contrasts. Specifically, this hypothesis posits that the difference in preferences between the low and the high magnitude condition will be significant when dominance between choice options is low but will be attenuated when dominance is high. As figure 27 shows, medium magnitude indeed had a negative effect on the likelihood of choosing the premium reward when comparing responses of participants of both low dominance groups ($M_{\text{mm-low}} = 4.59$ versus $M_{\text{mm-high}} = 3.16$, $t(97) = 3.19$, $p < .01$). According to expectations, this medium magnitude effect was not observed when considering the high dominance conditions ($M_{\text{mm-low}} = 3.15$ versus $M_{\text{mm-high}} = 2.78$, $t(95) = .85$, n.s). Hence, as hypothesized, high dominance between choice options constitutes a boundary condition of the impact of medium magnitude on reward decisions.

Figure 27. The Effect of Medium Magnitude and Dominance between Choice Options on the Likelihood of Redeeming a Premium Ticket over a Standard Ticket

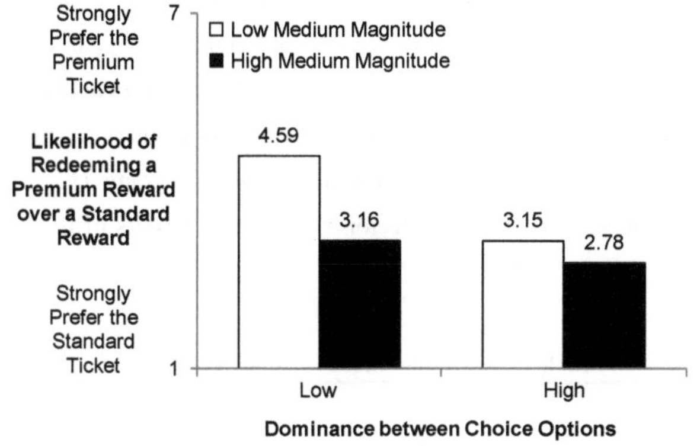

4.3 Study 12

4.3.1 Participants, Design, and Procedure

Finally, the purpose of study 12 is to confirm the external validity of the identified negative effect of medium magnitude on the likelihood of redeeming higher priced premium rewards. To this end, the customer survey about perceptions of and behavior in real-world loyalty programs—already used in study 6—provides the data base for the following analysis. In addition to the already described measures, the questionnaire also asked participants to indicate whether they had previously redeemed a reward in the loyalty program they were most familiar with and—if the question was answered in the affirmative—the monetary value of the latest redeemed reward. The responses of 292 participants who indicated that they already redeemed a reward were used for analysis.[13]

[13] The characteristics of the subsample used for analysis marginally differ from the structure of the total sample accessed in study 6. The majority of subjects (M_{age} = 33.0 years, SD_{age} = 13.4, 58.6% female) was employed or self-employed (47.7%) followed by students (38.7%); retired and unemployed participants as well as homemakers account for 13.7 percent of the sample.

4.3.2 Results

To validate the negative effect of medium magnitude on premium reward preferences, regression analysis with the monetary value of the latest redeemed reward as an approximation for the likelihood of redeeming a premium reward was performed. Thereby, the monetary value of the latest redeemed reward was regressed on perceptions of medium magnitude of the most familiar loyalty program and the control variables of price consciousness, attractiveness of rewards, duration of participation, and attitude towards loyalty programs ($F(5, 283) = 4.81$, $p < .01$, $R^2 = .08$, highest variance inflation factor = 1.05). The results of the estimation of regression coefficients appear in table 25.

Table 25. Regression Results of Study 12

	β	*t*	*p*
Main Effect			
Medium Magnitude	−.14	2.47	< .05
Covariates			
Perceived Attractiveness of Rewards	.18	3.14	< .01
Price Consciousness	−.04	.69	n.s.
Duration of Participation	.17	3.13	< .01
Attitude toward Loyalty Programs	−.05	.87	n.s.

As can be seen in table 25, medium magnitude had a significant negative impact on the value of redeemed rewards ($\beta = -.14$, $t = 2.47$, $p < .05$). This finding provides further evidence for the proposed medium magnitude effect on reward decisions. In addition, the dependent variable was positively affected by perceived attractiveness of rewards ($\beta = .18$, $t = 3.14$, $p < .01$) and duration of participation ($\beta = .17$, $t = 3.13$, $p < .01$). However, the low R^2 value indicates that the monetary value of redeemed rewards also depends on other variables to a significant extent which were not incorporated into the estimated regression model.

To better understand the strength of the medium magnitude effect on reward decisions, the sample's median of the perception of medium magnitude (4.00) was used to separate low (≤ 4.00, $M_{mm\text{-}low} = 2.94$, $n = 141$) from high (> 4.00, $M_{mm\text{-}high} = 5.86$, $n = 151$) medium magnitude groups. The results of a t-test confirmed that participants in the low magnitude group redeemed rewards with an average monetary value of €30.88, whereas rewards of those in the high magnitude group exhibited an average value of only €25.30 ($t = 1.89$, $p < .10$). Hence, the monetary value of the latest redeemed reward of respondents who perceived the medium magnitude of their most familiar loyalty program as high was 18.1 percent lower relative to those respondents whose rating of the perception of medium magnitude of the loyalty program under consideration was low.

4.4 Discussion

In summary, the above series of studies provide support of the proposed medium magnitude effect on the choice between different rewards and its boundary condition. Individuals apparently use the nominal differences in the prices of rewards to evaluate the desirability of premium rewards relative to standard rewards and—since these differences are perceived as larger in high magnitude programs than in low magnitude programs—premium reward preferences decline with increasing medium magnitude.

With regards to study 10, the examined loyalty programs differed in terms of their level of medium magnitude and, consequently, in the nominal number of extra loyalty points which have to be abandoned when redeeming a premium reward instead of a standard reward. However, since the provided rewards in both programs required exactly the same effort—i.e. the same monetary amount spent on the company—these nominal differences should not, from a rational perspective, affect choice. Nonetheless, this study demonstrates that individuals tend to misvalue the real additional costs of redeeming a premium instead of a standard reward. More precisely, the high nominal differences in the number of points required to redeem a premium instead of a standard reward which are associated with a high magnitude program currency lead to higher perceived prices of premium rewards relative to standard rewards even though actual differences in terms of additional required effort to obtain premium rewards remain the same. In other words, a high magnitude design entails that the price premium required to redeem a premium reward is overvalued such that these rewards appear more expensive relative to standard rewards and, consequently, are less likely to be chosen (H3b).

Study 11 broadens the understanding of the medium magnitude effect on reward decisions by investigating the moderating role of dominance structures between choice options. This study confirms hypothesis 4b which postulates that the negative effect of medium magnitude on premium reward preferences is only present in case of low dominance between the reward options under consideration. Therefore, varying the dominance structure between available rewards by increasing the price of the premium reward diminishes the relative weight w of incorporating the irrelevant nominal price differences into decision-making, such that reward decisions remain unaffected by medium magnitude.

Finally, study 12 examines the relationship between perceptions of medium magnitude in real-world loyalty programs and the monetary value of redeemed rewards. Using this monetary value as approximation for the quality of the rewards chosen, this investigation provides additional support for the hypothesized negative medium magnitude effect on the likelihood of redeeming a premium reward. However, perceptions of the number of points required for redemption in existing programs might additionally be influenced by other program characteristics such as, in particular, redemption thresholds. Nonetheless, the results of this study are in line with hypothesis 3b and, thus, can be understood as a demonstration of the external validity of the experimental findings of both study 10 and study 11. In conclusion, the studies presented in this chapter highlight that the proposed medium magnitude effect on reward decisions is evident among different contexts, sample structures, and methods of analysis.

E Conclusions

This thesis has presented a theoretical foundation and an empirical investigation of medium magnitude effects on consumer decisions in loyalty program memberships. To provide the basis for a purposeful deduction of conclusions, the following chapter 1 summarizes the central empirical findings. In a second step, both theoretical (chapter 2) as well as managerial implications (chapter 3) are discussed. A subsequent outline of limitations and future research directions (chapter 4) concludes this dissertation.

1 Summary of Findings

Loyalty programs have become a popular instrument for improving customer loyalty and have been widely adopted by marketers in diverse business branches. This dissertation documents systematic differences in consumer decisions in loyalty program memberships due to the specification of the magnitude of a loyalty program medium which solely influences the value of loyalty points in nominal but not in real terms.

Specifically, considering the effects of medium magnitude on participation decisions and redemption decisions, the empirical findings indicate that medium magnitude effects are paradoxically asymmetric. Even though a high medium magnitude has a positive impact on the likelihood of joining a loyalty program, it negatively affects the likelihood of redeeming hereupon accumulated points. The investigation of purchase and reward decisions reveals a similar asymmetry. While the preference for buying higher priced premium products increases with a program's medium magnitude, the preference for premium rewards declines. Hence, high magnitude program currencies seem to be associated with higher perceived values promoting its collection but constraining its spending. In this dissertation, two complementary explanations for this phenomenon are offered.

First, the S-shaped form of the prospect theory's (Kahneman and Tversky 1979) value function—i.e. concave for gains and convex for losses—suggests that segregated gains are associated with higher perceived values than integrated gains whereas, conversely, losses loom larger in case of segregation than in case of integration (Thaler 1985). Transferring these principles to the loyalty program context suggests that—when compared to low magnitude programs—a high magnitude program currency which is characterized by a large number of points, each with a low value, reflects the idea of segregation of both gains and losses; entailing higher value perceptions in decisions related to point accumulation, i.e. participation and purchase decisions, and, due to more pronounced perceptions of losses, reluctant point spending behavior in redemption and reward decisions. Second, the anchoring and adjustment heuristic (Tversky and Kahneman 1974) provides an additional explanation for medium magnitude effects on consumer choices. Based on this approach, it is expected that individuals use the nominal number of points credited for purchases and required for redemption as an initial anchor when evaluating the available choice options. Since final judgments are typically biased toward anchor values, large nominal amounts of issued points stimulate medium collection and, thus, influence participation and purchase decisions in favor of the program hosting company, while insufficient adjustment of high nominal prices of program incentives hinders reward redemption.

Moreover, the identified effects of dominance structures between choice options in each of the four decision fields under consideration contributes to a better understanding as to when and why program members rely on the irrelevant nominal number of points rather than their real values. In particular, if dominance between choice alternatives is ambiguous, the magnitude of a loyalty program currency strongly influences choice; in contrast, its impact disappears if the examination of dominance structures yields clearly superior choice options. These findings are consistent with the concept of reason-based choice (Shafir et al. 1993; Simonson 1989). According to this approach people seek for good reasons for the choices they make. Insights from the reported studies affirm that when faced with equally attractive choice alternatives—as is the case in the absence of a clear dominance structure between choice options—people attempt to reach a reasonable choice by including the irrelevant specification of medium magnitude into decision-making.

In addition, in support of the external validity of the presented findings, the studies reveal that the impact of medium magnitude on loyalty program members' decisions is robust among different data collection methods, program contexts, sample structures, and methods of analysis.

2 Theoretical Implications

This dissertation raises several theoretical implications to different streams of literature. First, this thesis contributes to the large body of research on loyalty programs. Despite the abundance of extant literature on this relationship instrument, previous research on medium characteristics is rather scarce. However, studies addressing medium issuance and redemption mechanisms indicate that alleged irrelevant specifications of medium characteristics are able to influence both consumer perceptions of such program schemes (Bagchi and Li 2011) and choice behavior (e.g., Kivetz et al. 2006; Nunes and Drèze 2006a; van Osselaer et al. 2004) remarkably. This dissertation enriches our knowledge by highlighting the impact of a previously neglected medium characteristic on customers' choices.

Second, although the theory of rational choice might provide an appropriate framework for prescribing how rational decision makers should decide, an abundance of empirical research on individual decision-making evidences deviations from rational behavior due to systematic violations of its underlying assumptions. In this vein, the documented medium magnitude effects contravene one of the most fundamental principles of rational choice; namely, the principle of invariance, which demands that preferences among different choice options are independent of their representation and, thereby, that different descriptions of the same choice problem which do not affect actual outcomes yield identical decisions (e.g., Bettman, Luce, and Payne 1998; Kahneman and Tversky 1984; Tversky 1996; Tversky and Kahneman 1986). Since the magnitude of a loyalty program currency neither affects the outcomes associated with available choice options nor their required efforts per se, the invariance principle precludes the occurrence of the detected effects. Therefore, medium magnitude effects align with other phenomena contradicting this principle—e.g., framing effects (e.g., Kahneman and Tversky 1979, 1984; Tversky and Kahneman 1981), the prominence effect (e.g., Fischer et al. 1999; Tversky et al. 1988), as well as the status quo bias (e.g., Ritov and Baron 1992; Samuelson and Zeckhauser 1988)—and, thus, contribute to a better understanding as to when and why people systematically deviate from rational choice behavior.

Third, this dissertation also enriches our knowledge regarding phenomena closely related to medium magnitude effects. According to extant literature on the phenomenon of medium maximization (Hsee et al. 2003; Nunes and Drèze 2006), individuals, when making decisions involving a medium between efforts and outcomes, often fail to accurately assess the relation between costs and final returns since they tend to overweight the medium/effort ratio relative to the outcome/medium ratio. However, previous research on this effect has merely compared choices involving a medium with non-medium control conditions while neglecting the effect of medium magnitude. Extending previous findings, the reported studies reveal that the medium maximization phenomenon also occurs as a consequence of varying magnitudes of loyalty program currencies. More precisely, the reported investigations of participation decisions indicate that high magnitude programs which exhibit a high medium/effort return—when compared to low magnitude programs—are associated with a higher likelihood of joining the program. Similarly, considering purchase decisions among standard and premium products, the relation between the extra number of points earned when buying a premium product relative to its additional monetary costs is larger in high magnitude programs entailing an increased preference for such higher priced offerings. Hence, in line with medium maximization research, the reported studies imply that a high magnitude program medium is perceived as more attractive due to its striking medium/effort relation; despite its comparatively unattractive reward/medium ratio. In other words, when making participation and purchase decisions, customers strongly focus on accumulating points rather than to the reward obtained in the end. Moreover, the examinations of medium magnitude effects on redemption and reward decisions provide further new insights; namely, in these decision contexts the outcome/medium ratio seems to outweigh the medium/effort relation—note that, the latter was essential for participation and purchase decisions. Hence, when it comes to medium spending decisions, the relative importance of both ratios seems to reverse, such that people aim to maximize the outcome/medium ratio while disregarding the medium/effort relation. In addition, this thesis follows a call for further research on situations where irrational medium effects appear and on an identification of their boundary conditions (Hsee et al. 2003). The systematic analyses of dominance structures between choice options shed light on the interplay between relevant and irrelevant information on decision-making and, thereby, explain as to when and why the irrelevant nominal number of loyalty points leads to biased decisions.

Furthermore, this dissertation's findings add to research on money illusion and the face value effect. Money illusion literature (Fehr and Tyran 2001; Fisher 1928; Shafir et al. 1997) suggests that individuals, when evaluating financial transactions, tend to focus on nominal rather than on adjusted real values. However, existing research on this phenomenon is still relatively scarce (Wertenbroch et al. 2007). In line with previous money illusion literature, the reported studies throughout demonstrate that consumers' evaluations of loyalty program related transactions are indeed influenced by nominal values of loyalty points. In addition, beyond existing money illusion research, this dissertation offers a novel theoretical explanation of this phenomenon. The results of this thesis suggest that money illusion does not merely arise because it is easier to think in nominal rather than in real terms (Shafir et al. 1997), but also because people use nominal values additionally to real values as further information for judgments. Furthermore, this research implicates that there might be situations where the money illusion phenomenon disappears. In a similar vein, the present dissertation confirms and extends findings of research on face value effects on spending behavior when using foreign currencies by following Wertenbroch et al.'s (2007) call for an investigation of related phenomena in a loyalty program context. The documented studies on redemption decisions affirm that loyalty program members tend to underspend if the loyalty program currency is more numerous (Raghubir and Srivastava 2002). In addition, the examination of the choice between different rewards indicates that people—similar to shopping situations involving foreign currencies (Wertenbroch et al. 2007)—compare the nominal number of loyalty points required to redeem alternative rewards such that the perceived price premium of premium rewards ascends with an increasing magnitude of a loyalty program currency. However, a major gap in previous research on the face value effect is that it merely concentrates on customers' spending behavior. In this regard, the present dissertation suggests that face value effects might also appear in situations where people acquire currencies (e.g., exchanging money for holiday trips or working abroad).

Finally, this dissertation contributes to the field of numerosity effects (e.g., Burson et al. 2009; Pandelaere et al. 2011; Pelham et al. 1994). Previous research in this domain often ascribes the effects resulting from providing the same information in different scale units (e.g., 365 days, 12 months, 1 year) on biased anchoring and adjustment processes. This research extends our understanding by offering an additional explanation of such effects by employing the concepts of integration and segregation. Such an additional explanation is particularly useful as several of the reported studies reveal that anchoring and insufficient adjustment cannot completely account for biased choices in loyalty program memberships.

3 Managerial Implications

Due to the high interchangeability of companies in various branches (e.g., retailing, airlines, financial services, etc.), the application of loyalty programs becomes a critical instrument to increase customer retention. This research's findings generate a better understanding of how the magnitude of a loyalty program currency influences the four key decisions fields in program memberships and, thus, supply important implications for a more efficient usage of such programs in business practices. Especially due to the fact that variations in the magnitude of a program medium have to be considered as cost neutral, the following recommendations should be of great interest for companies planning to develop and implement a loyalty program as well as for firms which already launched a loyalty scheme.

3.1 Influencing Participation and Redemption Decisions

First, considering participation decisions, the reported studies indicate that the acquisition of new members for a loyalty program can be realized in two ways. Most obviously, companies can improve participation rates among their customer bases by enhancing their customers' perceptions of program benefits relative to the costs required to obtain them. Variations of a program's outcome/effort ratio can be implemented, for instance, by increasing the value or attractiveness of the offered rewards, reducing redemption thresholds, and increasing ease of point collection. Aside from this plausible driver of program participation, the results of this dissertation imply that program providers should feature loyalty program currencies with a preferably high magnitude for the purpose of improving program penetration. Such a high magnitude medium is especially effective in attracting new members for programs which are characterized by a relatively low outcome/effort ratio. Although changes in the specification of the magnitude of an existing program's currency might be difficult to enforce, providers of existing programs can also benefit from this dissertation's findings. For instance, the finding that medium magnitude effects unfold their full potential if a program's outcome/effort ratio is low, existing high magnitude programs struggling with cost effectiveness issues could increase redemption thresholds without fearing a substantial drop of participation rates.

Second, with regard to redemption decisions, the presented results suggest that the prices of rewards in high magnitude programs are systematically overvalued holding the risk of low redemption intentions. From the company's perspective, this is both good and bad news. On the one hand, a high magnitude program is less cost-intensive as members participate to gain rather than to redeem points. On the other hand, such a program might lose its attractiveness in the long run and lead to frustration if customers do not exchange their accumulated points for rewards (Stauss et al. 2005; Nunes and Drèze 2006b). In addition, redemption has been shown to cause rewarded behavior effects (e.g., Taylor and Neslin 2005) reflected in favorable changes of purchase patterns. Consequently, such a reinforcement of loyal purchase behavior is expected to be stronger in lower magnitude programs not hindering reward redemption.

However, since medium magnitude effects disappear with the existence of clear dominance structures among available choice alternatives, redemption behavior in high magnitude programs can be enhanced by increasing the dominance between choice options in the redemption decision context—i.e. between redemption and non-redemption. For instance, similar to findings on the asymmetric dominance and compromise effect (e.g., Huber et al. 1982; Simonson 1989; Simonson and Tversky 1992), this can be realized by introducing disproportionately expensive 'decoy' rewards making redemption superior to non-redemption in terms of saving loyalty points toward future redemption goals.

3.2 Influencing Purchase and Reward Decisions

Aside from medium magnitude effects on participation and redemption decisions, the presented results reveal that program hosting companies can influence their customers' choice between products or services of different quality in both purchase and reward decisions by means of the specification of medium magnitude of their loyalty schemes.

First, the intention to increase sales of higher priced premium products among loyalty program members can be enforced via a high medium magnitude design which significantly improves the likelihood of buying a premium product instead of a standard product. The incentive in terms of earned loyalty points for buying a premium product instead of a standard product is perceived as larger in high magnitude programs and, thus, enhances the participants' preference for these products. However, the effectiveness of this implementation strategy is solely proved if the offered standard and premium products are similar attractive regarding their outcome/input ratio. Hence, if a company's premium products' prices cannot be justified by commensurate higher value perceptions, favorable medium magnitude effects may vanish.

Second, reward decisions have been shown to be affected by medium magnitude as well. In this regard, a high magnitude program design has been evidenced to induce hesitation regarding point spending. Since the price premium of redeeming premium rewards instead of standard rewards is perceived as larger in high magnitude programs people seem to be rather reluctant regarding point spending on premium rewards. Hence, program members appear to become more 'price' conscious and, thus, feel uncomfortable paying seemingly higher prices for premium rewards. Therefore, if companies operating a high magnitude program wish to remunerate loyal customers with premium rewards, they should reduce their premium reward prices to increase their relative attractiveness. On the other hand, companies which simply aim to increase redemption rates to benefit from rewarded behavior effects (e.g., Taylor and Neslin 2005) should increase premium reward prices remaining premium reward preferences low but increasing dominance of redemption over future redemption and, thereby, enhancing redemption rates. In addition, companies operating low magnitude programs might consider increasing the prices of premium rewards, since program members are willing to spend a less numerous price premium for redeeming premium rewards. This may have positive effects on the cost effectiveness of a program.

3.3 Additional Fields of Application

Despite the focus of this dissertation on loyalty programs, its findings might additionally be applicable to other situations involving a medium. For instance, student exams where points are earned for every exercise typically involve such a mechanism. From a normative perspective, it should be irrelevant whether an exercise credits 10 points out of 40 or 20 out of 80. However, students' motivation to collect points and, thereby, results may diverge. In addition, magnitude effects may arise for distances and sizes (e.g., expressed in centimeters, inches, meters, or kilometers) as well as for durations (e.g., expressed in minutes versus hours) or weights (e.g., expressed in gram versus kilogram). For instance, there might be unequal perceptions of television sets whose display size is either expressed in inches or in centimeters or taxi fares might be perceived to be a better value for money when reporting the traveled distance in meters rather than in kilometers. Finally, since the money earned from work also represents a medium (Hsee et al. 2003), this research's findings might also contribute to an explanation of individual consumption and saving behavior in times of inflation—given that inflation affects both incomes and prices. For instance, the presented results are in line with the paradoxical positive relationship between price inflation and saving rates (e.g., Juster and Taylor 1975; Howard 1978).

4 Limitations and Future Research Directions

This dissertation sheds light on previously neglected effects of the specification of the magnitude of a loyalty program currency which constitutes an important parameter of medium issuance and redemption mechanisms. The reported studies provide a purposeful examination of medium magnitude effects on the key decisions in program memberships and, furthermore, uncover a wide range of new research avenues.

First, within each of the constructed experiments or choice problems, the magnitude of the loyalty program currencies under consideration was merely varied among two levels—i.e. low and high—rendering an analysis of non-linear relationships between the level of medium magnitude and customer decisions impossible. Hence, an investigation of the nature of the impact of medium magnitude on program members' choices and, in this context, an examination if and when medium magnitude effects exceed their maximum might become subject to future investigations.

Second, aside from studying the main effects of medium magnitude on choice behavior this thesis is centered toward an examination of the moderating role of dominance structures between the available choice options in each of the four decision fields. Future research should explore additional factors which influence the extent to which the, normatively irrelevant, specification of medium magnitude affects decision-making. For instance, the loyalty programs described in the conducted studies were generally characterized by an exchange rate between purchases and earned loyalty points as well as between points and rewards which made the calculation of the number of purchases required to redeem a reward relatively easy. However, loyalty schemes in business practices often hinder a simple derivation of the relationship between requisite inputs and outcomes by employing more complex medium issuance and redemption structures. Hence, this complexity might be an additional moderator of medium magnitude effects which should be addressed by future studies.

Third, the presented studies have shown that high magnitude programs entail favorable consumer reactions in terms of participation and purchase decisions. However, such a program design hinders point redemption. This dissertation shows that the negative effects disappear with increasing dominance between choice options in the redemption decision context. However, as reward redemption is a critical facet of the attractiveness of a loyalty program (Nunes and Drèze 2006b; Stauss et al. 2005) and enhances loyal purchase patterns (Taylor and Neslin 2005), future research should pay special attention to an exploration of how a high medium magnitude program should be designed to make redemption for customers as pleasant as possible. In a similar vein, it should be investigated if people behave reluctant when it comes to redemption in high magnitude programs because they already perceive the high amounts of points in their accounts as some kind of reward.

Fourth, previous research on medium issuance and redemption mechanism has identified phenomena caused by, from a rational perspective, irrelevant variations of medium characteristics. Future research might combine the findings of this dissertation with existing knowledge and should, for instance, explore whether the endowed progress effect (Kivetz et al. 2006; Nunes and Drèze 2006b) is more pronounced in high than in low magnitude programs. In addition, the combined effects of non-linear medium issuance structures and medium magnitude on consumer choices might be worth a closer investigation (van Osselaer et al. 2004).

Fifth, whereas this thesis concentrates on the effects of medium magnitude on the key decisions loyalty program members make, other consequences are conceivable. For instance, Bagchi and Li (2011) already demonstrated that medium magnitude influences post-enrollment inferences in terms of perceptions of progress. Additional research might focus on the effects of medium magnitude on perceptions of status (e.g., Drèze and Nunes 2009). More specifically, it might be interesting to examine whether status perceptions are enhanced when a specific status level is attained after accumulating 1,000 points rather than after collecting 10 points though the required purchase volume remains constant. In this regard, similar to quality inferences by means of product prices (Zeithaml 1988), medium magnitude might influence the perceived value of rewards, such that a specific reward appears more valuable when it is priced at 1,000 points of a high magnitude currency than at 10 points of a low magnitude currency.

Finally, the presented results are predominantly based on controlled, scenario-based experimental conditions. To some degree, this empirical approach limits that conclusions can be transferred to real-world loyalty programs. Although the customer survey about loyalty program members' perceptions of and behavior in existing loyalty programs used in study 6 and study 12 already addresses this issue, future research may additionally use real data of customers' actual behavior. Especially, the wide application fields of implications resulting from research on medium magnitude effects—in excess of loyalty program designs—should encourage future research to gain deeper insight into this phenomenon.

References

Agresti, Alan, Dennis Wackerly, and James M. Boyett (1979), "Exact Conditional Tests for Cross-Classifications: Approximation of Attained Significance Levels," *Psychometrika*, 44 (1), 75–83.

Aiken, Leona S. and Stephen G. West (1991), *Multiple Regression: Testing and Interpreting Interactions*, Newbury Park, CA: Sage.

Ailawadi, Kusum L., Scott A. Neslin, and Karen Gedenk (2001), "Pursuing the Value-Conscious Consumer: Store Brands Versus National Brand Promotions," *Journal of Marketing*, 65 (1), 71–89.

Allaway, Arthur W., David Berkowitz, and Giles D'Souza (2003), "Spatial Diffusion of a New Loyalty Program through a Retail Market," *Journal of Retailing*, 79 (3), 137–151.

Anderson, Eugene W., Claes Fornell, and Donald R. Lehmann (1994), "Customer Satisfaction, Market Share, and Profitability: Findings From Sweden," *Journal of Marketing*, 58 (July), 53–66.

Arbore, Alessandro and Zachary Estes (2013), "Loyalty Program Structure and Consumers' Perceptions of Status: Feeling Special in a Grocery Store?" *Journal of Retailing and Consumer Services*, 20 (5), 439–444.

Ariely, Dan and Thomas S. Wallsten (1995), "Seeking Subjective Dominance in Multidimensional Space: An Explanation of the Asymmetric Dominance Effect," *Organizational Behavior and Human Decision Processes*, 63 (3), 223–232.

Arkes, Hal R., Cynthia A. Joyner, Mark V. Pezzo, Jane Gradwohl Nash, Karen Siegel-Jacobs, and Eric Stone (1994), "The Psychology of Windfall Gains," *Organizational Behavior and Human Decision Processes*, 59 (3), 331–347.

Arrow, Kenneth J. (1982), "Risk Perception in Psychology and Economics," *Economic Inquiry*, 20 (1), 1–9.

Arrow, Kenneth J. and Gerard Debreu (1954), "Existence of an Equilibrium for a Competitive Economy," *Econometrica*, 22 (3), 265–290.

Ashley, Christy, Stephanie M. Noble, Naveen Donthu, and Katherine N. Lemon (2011), "Why Customers Won't Relate: Obstacles to Relationship Marketing Engagement," *Journal of Business Research*, 64 (7), 749–756.

Bagchi, Rajesh and Xingbo Li (2011), "Illusionary Progress in Loyalty Programs: Magnitudes, Reward Distances, and Step-Size Ambiguity," *Journal of Consumer Research*, 37 (5), 888–901.

Baron, Jonathan (2009), *Thinking and Deciding*, Cambridge, UK: Cambridge University Press.

Barone, Michael J. and Tirthankar Roy (2010), "The Effect of Deal Exclusivity on Consumer Response to Targeted Price Promotions: A Social Identification Perspective," *Journal of Consumer Psychology*, 20 (1), 78–89.

Ben-Akiva, Moshe and Steven R. Lerman (1985), *Discrete Choice Analysis: Theory and Application to Travel Demand*, Cambridge, MA: MIT Press.

Bettman, J., Luce, M. F. und Payne, J. W. (1998), "Constructive Consumer Choice Processes," *Journal of Consumer Research*, 25 (3), 187–217.

Berry, Jeff (2013), "Bulking Up: The 2013 Colloquy Loyalty Census: Growth and Trends in U.S. Loyalty Program Activity," Colloquy White Paper, Cincinnati, OH.

Birnbaum, Michael H. (1990), "A Theory of Comparative Response Times and 'Difference' Judgments," *Cognitive Psychology*, 22 (2), 184–210.

Bitner, Mary J. (1995), "Building Service Relationships: It's All About Promises," *Journal of the Academy of Marketing Science*, 23 (4), 246–251.

Blair, Edward and George M. Zinkhan (2006), "Nonresponse and Generalizability in Academic Research," *Journal of the Academy of Marketing Science*, 34 (1), 4–7.

Bolton, Ruth N., R. K. Kannan, and Matthew D. Bramlett (2000), "Implications of Loyalty Program Membership and Service Experiences for Customer Retention and Value," *Journal of the Academy of Marketing Science*, 28 (1), 95–108.

Börsch-Supan, Axel (1987), Econometric Analysis of Discrete Choice, Berlin, Germany: Springer.

Bradley, Ralph A. and Milton E. Terry (1952), "Rank Analysis of Incomplete Block Designs: I. The Method of Paired Comparisons," *Biometrika*, 39 (3/4), 324–345.

Brown, Christina L. and Gregory S. Carpenter (2000), "Why Is the Trivial Important? A Reasons-Based Account for the Effects of Trivial Attributes on Choice," *Journal of Consumer Research*, 26 (4), 372–385.

Burnham, Thomas A., Judy K. Frels, and Vijay Mahajan (2003), "Consumer Switching Costs: A Typology, Antecedents, and Consequences," *Journal of the Academy of Marketing Science*, 31 (2), 109–126.

Burson, Katherine A., Richard P. Larrick, and John G. Lynch (2009), "Six of One, Half Dozen of the Other – Expanding and Contracting Numerical Dimensions Produces Preference Reversals," *Psychological Science*, 20 (9), 1074–1078.

Calder, Bobby J., Lynn W. Phillips, and Alice M. Tybout (1981), "Designing Research for Application," *Journal of Consumer Research*, 8 (2), 197–207.

Camerer, Colin F. and George Loewenstein (2004), "Behavioral Economic: Past, Present, Future," in *Advances in Behavioral Economics*, eds. Colin F. Camerer, George Loewenstein, and Matthew Babin, Princeton, NJ: Princeton University Press, 3–51.

Campbell, Donald T. and Julian C. Stanley (1963), *Experimental and Quasi-Experimental Designs for Research*, Chicago, IL: Rand McNally.

Carlsson, Fredrik and Åsa Löfgren (2006), "Airline Choice, Switching Costs and Frequent Flyer Programmes," *Applied Economics*, 38 (13), 1469–1475.

Carmon, Ziv and Dan Ariely (2000), "Focusing on the Forgone: How Value Can Appear So Different to Buyers and Sellers," *Journal of Consumer Research*, 27 (3), 360–370.

Carmon, Ziv and Itamar Simonson (1998), "Price–Quality Trade-Offs in Choice Versus Matching: New Insights Into the Prominence Effect," *Journal of Consumer Psychology*, 7 (4), 323–343.

Carpenter, Gregory S., Rashi Glazer, and Ken Nakamoto (1994), "Meaningful Brands from Meaningless Differentiation: The Dependence on Irrelevant Attributes," *Journal of Marketing Research*, 31 (3), 339–350.

Chapman, Gretchen B. and Eric J. Johnson (1994), "The Limits of Anchoring," *Journal of Behavioral Decision Making*, 7 (4), 223–242.

Chapman, Gretchen B. and Eric J. Johnson (1999), "Anchoring, Activation, and the Construction of Values," *Organizational Behavior and Human Decision Processes*, 79 (2), 115–153.

Connolly, Terry and Jochen Reb (2012), "Toward Interactive, Internet-Based Decision Aid for Vaccination Decisions: Better Information Alone is Not Enough," *Vaccine*, 30 (25), 3813–3818.

Cortiñas, Mónica, Margarita Elorz, and José Miguel Múgica (2008), "The Use of Loyalty-Cards Databases: Differences in Regular Price and Discount Sensitivity in the Brand Choice Decision between Card and Non-Card Holders," *Journal of Retailing and Consumer Services*, 15 (1), 52–62.

Cronbach, Lee J. (1951), Coefficient Alpha and the Internal Structure of Tests, *Psychometrika*, 16 (3), 297–334.

Debreu, Gerard (1960), "Topological Methods in Cardinal Utility Theory," in *Mathematical Methods in the Social Sciences*, eds. Kenneth J. Arrow, Samule Karlin, and Patrick Suppes, Stanford, CA: Stanford University Press, 16–26.

Deighton, John (2000), "Frequency Programs in Service Industries," in *Handbook of Services Marketing and Management*, T. Swartz and D. Iacobucci, eds. London: Sage Publications, 401–408.

Demoulin, Nathalie T. M. and Pietro Zidda (2009), "Drivers of Customers' Adoption and Adaption Timing of a New Loyalty Card," *Journal of Retailing*, 85 (3), 391–405.

Desmet, Pierre (2002), "A Study of the Potential Effects of the Conversion to Euro," *Journal of Product and Brand Management*, 11 (3), 134–46.

De Cannièrea, Marie Hélène, Patrick De Pelsmacker, and Maggie Geuens (2009), "Relationship Quality and the Theory of Planned Behavior models of behavioral intentions and purchase behavior," *Journal of Business Research*, 62 (1), 82–92.

De Wulf, Kristof, Gaby Odekerken-Schröder, Marie Hélène de Cannière, and Claudia Van Oppen (2003), "What Drives Consumer Participation to Loyalty Programs? A Conjoint Analytical Approach," *Journal of Relationship Marketing*, 2 (1/2), 69–83.

De Wulf, Kristof, Gaby Odekerken-Schröder, and Dawn Iacobucci (2001), "Investments in Consumer Relationships: A Cross-Country and Cross-Industry Exploration," *Journal of Marketing*, 65 (4), 33–50.

Dhar, Ravi and Klaus Wertenbroch (2000), "Consumer Choice Between Hedonic and Utilitarian Goods," *Journal of Marketing Research*, 37 (1), 60–71.

Dholakia, Utpal M. (2006), "How Customer Self-Determination Influences Relational Marketing Outcomes: Evidence from Longitudinal Field Studies," *Journal of Marketing Research*, 43 (1), 109–120.

Donthu, Naveen and Adriana Garcia (1999), "The Internet Shopper", *Journal of Advertising research*, 39 (3), 52–58.

Dorotic, Matilda, Tammo H. A. Bijmolt, and Peter C. Verhoef, P.C. (2012), "Loyalty Programmes: Current Knowledge and Research Directions," *International Journal of Management Reviews*, 14 (3), 217–237.

Dowling, Grahame R. and Mark Uncles (1997), "Do Customer Loyalty Programs Really Work?" *Sloan Management Review*, 38 (Summer), 71–82.

Dowling, Grahame R., Mark Uncles, and Kathy Hammond (2003), "Customer Loyalty and Customer Loyalty Programs," *Journal of Consumer Marketing*, 20 (4), 294–316.

Drèze, Xavier and Stephen J. Hoch (1998), "Exploiting the Installed Base Using Cross-Merchandising and Category Destination Programs," *International Journal of Research in Marketing*, 15 (5), 459–471.

Drèze, Xavier and Joseph C. Nunes (2004), "Using Combined-Currency Prices to Lower Consumers' Perceived Cost," *Journal of Marketing Research*, 41 (February), 59–72.

Drèze, Xavier and Joseph C. Nunes (2007), "Recurring Goals: The Effect of Divisibility and Goal Attainment on Self-Efficacy and Effort," *Marshall Research Paper Series*, Working Paper MKT 07-07.

Drèze, Xavier and Joseph C. Nunes (2009), "Feeling Superior: The Impact of Loyalty Program Structure on Consumers' Perceptions of Status," *Journal of Consumer Research*, 35 (6), 890–905.

Drèze, Xavier and Joseph C. Nunes (2011), "Recurring Goals and Learning: The Impact of Successful Reward Attainment on Purchase Behavior," *Journal of Marketing Research*, 48 (2), 268–281.

Einhorn, Hillel J. (1970), "The Use of Nonlinear, Noncompensatory Models in Decision Making," *Psychological Bulletin*, 73 (3), 221–230.

Ewards, Ward (1954), "The Theory of Decision Making," *Psychological Bulletin*, 51(4), 380–417.

Ehrenberg, Andrew S. C., Gerald J. Goodhardt, and T. Patrick Barwise (1990), "Double Jeopardy Revisited," *Journal of Marketing*, 54 (3), 82–91.

Ehrenberg, Andrew S. C., Kathy Hammond, and Gerald J. Goodhardt (1994), "The After-Effects of Price-Related Consumer Promotions," *Journal of Advertising Research*, 34 (4), 11–21.

Eisinga, Rob, Manfred te Grotenhuis, and Ben Pelzer (2013), "The reliability of a two-item scale: Pearson, Cronbach, or Spearman-Brown?" *International Journal of Public Health*, 58 (4), 637–642.

Epley, Nicholas and Thomas Gilovich (2001), "Putting Adjustment Back in the Anchoring and Adjustment Heuristic: Differential Processing of Self-Generated and Experimenter-Provided Anchors," *Psychological Science*, 12 (5), 391–396.

Epley, Nicholas and Thomas Gilovich (2006), "The Anchoring-and-Adjustment Heuristic: Why the Adjustments Are Insufficient," *Psychological Science*, 17 (4), 311–318.

Epley, Nicholas, Boaz, Keysar, Leaf van Boven, and Thomas Gilovich (2004), "Perspective Taking as Egocentric Anchoring and Adjustment," *Journal of Personality and Social Psychology*, 87 (3), 327–339.

Erickson, Gary M. and Johny K. Johansson (1985), "The Role of Price in Multi-Attribute Product Evaluations," *Journal of Consumer Research*, 12 (2), 195–199.

Evanschitzky, Heiner, B. Ramaseshan, David M. Woisetschläger, Verena Richelsen, Markus Blut, and Christof Backhaus (2011), "Consequences of Customer Loyalty to the Loyalty Program and to the Company", *Journal of the Academy of Marketing Science*, 40 (5), 625–638.

Evanschitzky, Heiner and Maren Wunderlich (2006), "An Examination of Moderator Effects in the Four-Stage Loyalty Model," *Journal of Service Research*, 8 (4), 330–345.

Everitt, Brian S. (1992), *The Analysis of Contingency Tables*, Boca Raton, FL: CRC Press.

Fantino, Edmund and Jay N. Goldshmidt (2000), "Differences, Not Ratios, Control Choice in an Experimental Analogue to Foraging," *Psychological Science*, 11 (3), 229–233.

Fehr, Ernst and Jean-Robert Tyran (2001), "Does Money Illusion Matter?" *The American Economic Review*, 91 (5), 1239–1262.

Fischer, Gregory W., Ziv Carmon, Dan Ariely, and Gal Zauberman (1999), "Goal-Based Construction of Preferences: Task Goals and the Prominence Effect," *Management Science*, 45 (8), 1057–1075.

Fischer, Gregory W. and Scott A. Hawkins (1993), "Strategy Compatibility, Scale Compatibility, and the Prominence Effect," *Journal of Experimental Psychology: Human Perception and Performance*, 19 (3), 580–597.

Fishburn, Peter C. (1970), *Utility Theory for Decision Making*, New York, NY: Wiley.

Fisher, Irving (1928), *The Money Illusion*, New York, NY: Adelphi.

Fisher, Ronald A. (1954), *Statistical Methods for Research Workers*, Edinburgh, Scotland: Oliver and Boyd.

Friedlander, Myrna L. and Susan J. Stockman (1983), "Anchoring and Publicity Effects in Clinical Judgment," *Journal of Clinical Psychology*, 39 (4), 637–644.

Friedman, Milton and Leonard J. Savage (1948), "The Utility Analysis of Choices Involving Risk," *Journal of Political Economy*, 56 (4), 279–304.

Gómez, Blanca García, Ana M Gutiérrez Arranz and Jesús Gutiérrez Cillán (2012), "Drivers of Customer Likelihood to Join Grocery Retail Loyalty Programs. An Analysis of Reward Programs and Loyalty Cards," *Journal of Retailing and Consumer Services*, 19 (5), 492–500.

Gordon, Michael E., Allen Slade, and Neal Schmitt (1986), "The 'Science of the Sophomore' Revisited: from Conjecture to Empiricism," *Academy of Management Review*, 11 (1), 191–207.

Gourville, John T. (1998), "Pennies-a-Day: The Effect of Temporal Reframing on Transaction Evaluation," *Journal of Consumer Research*, 24 (4), 395–403.

Gourville, John T. and Dilip Soman (1998), "Payment Depreciation: The Behavioral Effects of Temporally Separating Payments from Consumption," *Journal of Consumer Research*, 25 (2), 160–174.

Graeff, Timothy R. and Susan Harmon (2002), "Collecting and Using Personal Data: Consumers' Awareness and Concerns," *Journal of Consumer Marketing*, 19 (4), 302–318.

Green, Paul E. (1973), "On the Analysis of Interactions in Marketing Research Data," *Journal of Marketing Research*, 10 (4), 410–420.

Greenberg, Jerald (1987), "The College Sophomore as Guinea Pig: Setting the Record Straight," *The Academy of Management Review*, 12 (1), 157–159.

Greenwald, Anthony G. (1976), "Within-Subjects Designs: To Use or Not To Use?" *Psychological Bulletin*, 83 (2), 314–320.

Gujarati, Damodar N. (2003), *Basic Econometrics*, New York, NY: McGraw-Hill.

Gwinner, Kevin P., Dwayne D. Gremler, and Mary J. Bitner (1998), "Relational Benefits in Services Industries: The Customer's Perspective," *Journal of the Academy of Marketing Science*, 26 (2), 101–114.

Hair, Joseph F., William C. Black, Barry J. Babin, and Rolph E. Anderson (2010), *Multi-variate Data Analysis*, Upper Saddle River, NJ: Pearson Prentice Hall.

Hair, Joseph F., Christian M. Ringle, and Marko Sarstedt (2011), "PLS-SEM: Indeed a Silver Bullet," *Journal of Marketing Theory and Practice*, 19 (2), 139–152.

Hansen, John D., George D. Deitz, and Robert M. Morgan (2010), "Taxonomy of Service-Based Loyalty Program Members," *Journal of Services Marketing*, 24 (4), 271–282.

Hardesty, David M., Jay P. Carlson, and William Bearden (2002), "Brand Familiarity and Invoice Price Effects on Consumer Evaluations: The Moderating Role of Skepticism toward Advertising," *Journal of Advertising*, 31 (2), 1–15.

Harman, Harry H. (1976), *Modern Factor Analysis*, Chicago, IL: University of Chicago Press.

Hartman, Raymond S., Michael J. Doane, and Chi-Keung Woo (1991), "Consumer Rationality and the Status Quo," *The Quarterly Journal of Economics*, 106 (1), 141–162.

Heath, Timothy B. and Subimal Chatterjee (1995), "Asymmetric Decoy Effects on Lower-Quality Versus Higher-Quality Brands: Meta-Analytic and Experimental Evidence," *Journal of Consumer Research*, 22 (3), 268–284.

Henderson, Conor M., Joshua T. Beck, and Robert W. Palmatier (2011), "Review of the Theoretical Underpinnings of Loyalty Programs," *Journal of Consumer Psychology*, 21 (3), 256–276.

Herne, Kaisa (1999), "The Effects of Decoy Gambles on Individual Choice," *Experimental Economics*, 2 (1), 31–40.

Herrnstein, Richard J. (1990), "Rational Choice Theory: Necessary but Not Sufficient," American Psychologist, 45 (3), 356–367.

Heskett, James L., W. Earl Sasser, and Leonard A. Schlesinger (1997), *The Service Profit Chain*, New York, NY: Free Press.

Highhouse, Scott (1996), "Context-Dependent Selection: The Effects of Decoy and Phantom Job Candidates," *Organizational Behavior and Human Decision Processes*, 65 (1), 68–76.

Howard, David H. (1978), "Personal Saving Behavior and the Rate of Inflation," *Review of Economics and Statistics*, 60 (4), 547–554.

Howard, Daniel J. and Roger A. Kerin (2006), "Broadening the Scope of Reference Price Advertising Research: A Field Study of Consumer Shopping Involvement," *Journal of Marketing*, 70 (4), 185–204.

Hsee, Christopher K. (1995), "Elastic Justification: How Tempting but Task-Irrelevant Factors Influence Decisions," *Organizational Behavior and Human Decision Processes*, 62 (3), 330–337.

Hsee, Christopher K., Fang Yu, Jiao Zhang, and Yan Zhang (2003), "Medium Maximization," *Journal of Consumer Research*, 30 (1), 1–14.

Hsee, Christopher K. and Jiao Zhang (2004), "Distinction Bias: Misprediction and Mischoice Due to Joint Evaluation," *Journal of Personality and Social Psychology*, 86 (5), 680–695.

Hsee, Christopher K., Jiao Zhang, Cindy F. Cai, and Shirley Zhang (2013), "Overearning," *Psychological Science*, 24 (6), 852–859.

Huber, Joel, John W. Payne, and Christopher Puto (1982), "Adding Asymmetrically Dominated Alternatives: Violations of Regularity and the Similarity Hypothesis," *Journal of Consumer Research*, 9 (1), 90–98.

Huber, Joel and Christopher Puto (1983), "Market Boundaries and Product Choice: Illustrating Attraction and Substitution Effects," *Journal of Consumer Research*, 10 (1), 31–44.

Hulin, Charles and Robert Cudeck (2001), "Cronbach's Alpha on Two-Item Scales," *Journal of Consumer Psychology*, 10 (1/2), 55–69.

Hulland, John (1999), "Use of Partial Least Squares (PLS) in Strategic Management Research: A Review of Four Recent Studies," *Strategic Management Journal*, 20 (2), 195–204.

Iyengar, Sheena S. and Mark R. Lepper (2000), "When Choice is Demotivating: Can One Desire too Much of a Good Thing?" *Journal of Personality and Social Psychology*, 79 (6), 995–1006.

Jang, Dongsuk and Anna S. Mattila (2005), "An Examination of Restaurant Loyalty Programs: What Kinds of Rewards Do Customers Prefer?" *International Journal of Contemporary Hospitality Management*, 17 (5), 402–408.

Johnson, Michael D., Andreas Herrmann, and Hans H. Bauer (1999), "The Effects of Price Bundling on Consumer Evaluations of Product Offerings," *International Journal of Research in Marketing*, 16 (2), 129–142.

Jonas, Eva, Tobias Greitemeyer, Dieter Frey, and Stefan Schulz-Hardt (2002), "Psychological Effects of the Euro—Experimental Research on The perception of Salaries and Price Estimations," *European Journal of Social Psychology*, 32 (2), 147–169.

Juster, F. Thomas and Lester D. Taylor (1975), "Towards a Theory of Saving Behavior," *American Economic Review*, 65 (2), 203–209.

Kahneman, Daniel, Jack L. Knetsch, and Richard H. Thaler (1990), "Experimental Tests of the Endowment Effect and the Coase-Theorem," *Journal of Political Economy*, 98 (6), 1325–1348.

Kahneman, Daniel, Jack L. Knetsch, and Richard H. Thaler (1991), "Anomalies: The Endowment Effect, Loss Aversion, and Status Quo Bias," *Journal of Economic Perspectives*, 5 (1), 193–206.

Kahneman, Daniel and Amos Tversky (1979), "Prospect Theory: An Analysis of Decision Under Risk," *Econometrica*, 47 (2), 263–291.

Kahneman, Daniel and Amos Tversky (1984), "Choices, Values, and Frames," *American Psychologist*, 39 (4), 341–350.

Kaicker, Ajit, William O. Bearden, and Kenneth C. Manning (1995), "Component versus Bundle Pricing: The Role of Selling Price Deviations from Price Expectations," *Journal of Business Research*, 33 (3), 231–239.

Kaplan, Robert M. and Dennis P. Saccuzo (1982), *Psychological Testing: Principles, Applications, and Issues*, Monterey, CA: Brooks/Cole.

Kassarjian, Harold H. (1971), "Personality and Consumer Behavior: A Review," *Journal of Marketing Research*, 8 (4), 409–418.

Keh, Hean Tat and Yih Hwai Lee (2006), "Do Reward Programs Build Loyalty for Services?: The Moderating Effect of Satisfaction on Type and Timing of Rewards," *Journal of Retailing*, 82 (2), 127–136.

Keppel, Geoffrey (1973), *Design and Analysis – A Researcher's Handbook*, Englewood Cliffs, NJ: Prentice-Hall.

Kim, Byung-Do, Mengze Shi, and Kannan Srinivasan (1997), "Colluding Through Capacity Reduction: A Rationale for Frequent Flyer Program." Working Paper, Carnegie Mellon University, Pittsburgh, PA.

Kim, Byung-Do, Mengze Shi, and Kannan Srinivasan (2001), "Reward Programs and Tacit Collusion," *Marketing Science*, 20 (2), 99–120.

Kirk, Roger E. (2013), *Experimental Design: Procedures for the Behavioral Sciences*, Thousand Oaks, CA: Sage.

Kivetz, Ran (2003), "The Effects of Effort and Intrinsic Motivation on Risky Choice," *Marketing Science*, 22 (4), S. 477–502.

Kivetz, Ran (2005), "Promotion Reactance: The Role of Effort-Reward Congruity," *Journal of Consumer Research*, 31 (4), 725–736.

Kivetz, Ran and Itamar Simonson (2002), "Earning the Right to Indulge: Effort as a Determinant of Customer Preferences Toward Frequency Program Rewards," *Journal of Marketing Research*, 39 (2), 155–170.

Kivetz, Ran and Itamar Simonson (2003), "The Idiosyncratic Fit Heuristic: Effort Advantage as a Determinant of Consumer Response to Loyalty Programs," *Journal of Marketing Research*, 40 (4), 454–467.

Kivetz, Ran, Oleg Urminsky, and Yuhuang Zheng (2006), "The Goal-Gradient Hypothesis Resurrected: Purchase Acceleration, Illusionary Goal Progress, and Customer Retention," *Journal of Marketing Research*, 43 (1), 39–58.

Kleinbaum, David E., Lawrence L. Kupper, and Keith E. Muller (1988), *Applied Regression Analysis and other Multivariate Methods*, Boston, MA: PWS-Kent.

Klemperer, Paul (1987), "The Competitiveness of Markets with Switching Costs," Rand *Journal of Economics*, 18 (1), 138–150.

Knetsch, Jack L., Fang-Fang Tang, and Richard H. Thaler (2001), "The Endowment Effect and Repeated Market Trials: Is the Vickrey Auction Demand Revealing?" *Experimental Economics*, 4 (3), 257–269.

Kopalle, Praveen K. and Scott A. Neslin (2003), "The Economic Viability of Frequency Reward Programs in a Strategic Competitive Environment," *Review of Marketing Science*, 1 (1), 1–39.

Kopalle, Praveen K., Scott A. Neslin, Baohong Sun, Yacheng Sun, and Vanitha Swaminathan (2007), "A Dynamic Structural Model of The Impact of Loyalty Programs on Customer Behavior," *Proceedings of the Marketing Dynamics Conference*.

Köcher, Sören and Markus Blut (2012), "Give-and-Take in Loyalty Programs: The Asymmetric Effect of Medium Magnitude," in *Summer Educators' Proceedings*, Vol. 23, eds. Todd J. Arnold and Lisa Scheer, Chicago, IL: American Marketing Association, 488–489.

Köcher, Sören and Markus Blut (2013a), "About the Relevance of Irrelevance: Does Medium Magnitude in Loyalty Programs Matter?" in *Summer Educators' Proceedings*, Vol. 24, eds. Rebecca Slotegraaf and David Griffith, Chicago, IL: American Marketing Association, 190–191.

Köcher, Sören and Markus Blut (2013b), "The Illusion of Points: Investigating the Effects of Medium Magnitude in Loyalty Programs," in *Proceedings of the 42nd European Marketing*

Academy Annual Conference, eds. Elif Karaosmanoğlu and A. Banu E. Baş, Brussels, Belgium: European Marketing Academy, 216.

Kristensen, Henrik and Tommy Gärling (1997), "The Effects of Anchor Points and Reference Points on Negotiation Process and Outcome," *Organizational Behavior and Human Decision Processes*, 71 (1), 85–94.

Kumar, Nanda and Ram Rao (2003), "Effect of Loyalty Card Programs on Supermarket Prices," Working Paper, School of Management, University of Texas at Dallas.

Kumar, V. and Denish Shah (2004), "Building and Sustaining Profitable Customer Loyalty for the 21st Century," *Journal of Retailing*, 80 (4), 317–329.

Lacey, Russel (2009), "Limited Influence of Loyalty Program Membership on Relational Outcomes," *Journal of Consumer Marketing*, 26 (6), 392–402.

Lacey, Russell and Julie Z. Sneath (2006), "Customer Loyalty Programs: Are They Fair to Consumers?" *Journal of Consumer Marketing*, 23 (7), 458–464.

Lal, Rajiv and David E. Bell (2003), "The Impact of Frequent Shopper Programs in Grocery Retailing," *Quantitative Marketing and Economics*, 1 (2), 179–202.

Latham, Gary P. and Edwin A. Locke (1991), "Self-Regulation through Goal Setting," Organizational Behavior and Human Decision Processes, 50 (2), 212–247.

Leenheer, Jorna (2004), *The Adoption and Effectiveness of Loyalty Programs in Retailing*, Tilburg University, the Netherlands: Center Dissertation Series.

Leenheer, Jorna and Tammo H.A. Bijmolt (2008), "Which Retailers Adopt a Loyalty Program? An Empirical Study," *Journal of Retailing and Consumer Services*, 15 (6), 429–442.

Leenheer, Jorna, Harald J. van Heerde, Tammo H.A. Bijmolt, and Ale Smidts (2007), "Do Loyalty Programs Really Enhance Behavioral Loyalty? An Empirical Analysis Accounting for Self-Selecting Members," *International Journal of Research in Marketing*, 24 (1), 31–47.

Lemon, Katherine N., Tiffany B. White, and Russell S. Winer (2002), "Dynamic Customer Relationship Management: Incorporating Future Considerations into the Service Retention Decision," *Journal of Marketing*, 66 (1), 1–14.

Lemon, Katherine N. and Florian von Wangenheim (2008), "The Reinforcing Effects of Loyalty Program Partnerships and Core Service Usage: A Longitudinal Analysis," *Journal of Service Research*, 11 (4), 357–370.

Levy, Jack S. (1992), "An Introduction to Prospect Theory," *Political Psychology*, 13 (2), 171–186.

Lewis, Michael (2004), "The Influence of Loyalty Programs and Short-Term Promotions on Customer Retention," *Journal of Marketing Research*, 41 (3), 281–292.

Li, Heng, Robert Rosenthal, and Donald B. Rubin (1996), "Reliability of Measurement in Psychology: From Spearman-Brown to Maximal Reliability," *Psychological Methods*, 1996, 1 (1), 98–107.

Li, Shu and Austin S. Adams (1995), "Is There Something More Important behind Framing?" *Organizational Behavior and Human Decision Processes*, 62 (2), 216–219.

Lichtenstein, Sarah and Paul Slovic (1971), "Reversals of Preference between Bids and Choices in Gambling Decisions," *Journal of Experimental Psychology*, 89 (1), 46–55.

Lichtenstein, Sarah and Paul Slovic (1973), "Response-Induced Reversals of Preference in Gambling: An Extended Replication in Las Vegas," *Journal of Experimental Psychology*, 101 (1), 16–20.

Lieber, Ron (2011), "All About Your Unused Rewards Points," *The New York Times*, April 19th, accessed May 12, 2014, [available at http://bucks.blogs.nytimes.com/ 2011/04/19/all-about-your-unused-rewards-points/?_r=0.]

Liebert, Robert M., William P. Smith, J. H. Hill, and Miriam Keiffer (1968), "The Effects of Information and Magnitude of Initial Offer on Interpersonal Negotiation," *Journal of Experimental Social Psychology*, 4 (4), 431–441.

Lim, Sonya S. (2006), "Do Investors Integrate Losses and Segregate Gains? Mental Accounting and Investor Trading Decisions," *Journal of Business*, 79 (5), 2539–2573.

Liston-Heyes, Catherine (2002), "Pie in the Sky? Real Versus Perceived Values of Air Miles," *Journal of Consumer Policy*, 25 (1), 1–26.

Liu, Matthew Tingchi and James L. Brock (2009), "Antecedents of Redemption of Reward Points: Credit Card Market in China and International Comparison," *Journal of International Consumer Marketing*, 22 (1), 33–45.

Liu, Yuping (2007), "The Long-Term Impact of Loyalty Programs on Consumer Purchase Behavior and Loyalty," *Journal of Marketing*, 71 (4), 19–35.

Liu, Yuping and Rong Yang (2009), "Competing Loyalty Programs: Impact of Market Saturation, Market Share, and Category Expandability," *Journal of Marketing*, 73 (1), 93–108.

Long, Mary M. and Leon G. Schiffman (2000), "Consumption Values and Relationships: Segmenting the Market for Frequency Programs," *Journal of Consumer Marketing*, 17 (3), 214–232.

Loomes, Graham and Caron Taylor (1992), "Non-Transitive Preferences Over Gains and Losses," *The Economic Journal*, 102 (411), 357–365.

Lowe, Ben, Bradley R. Barnes, and Robert Rugimbana (2012), "Discounting in International Markets and the Face Value Effect: A Double- Edged Sword?" *Psychology & Marketing*, 29 (3), 144–156.

Luce, R. Duncan (1959), *Individual Choice Behavior: A Theoretical Analysis*, New York, NY: Wiley.

Luce, R. Duncan and John W. Tukey (1964), "Simultaneous Conjoint Measurement: A New Type of Fundamental Measurement," *Journal of Mathematical Psychology*, 1 (1), 1–27.

Lynch, John G. (1982), "On the External Validity of Experiments in Consumer Research," *Journal of Consumer Research*, 9 (3), 225–239.

Malhotra, Naresh K. (2010), *Marketing Research*, Upper Saddle River, NJ: Pearson Prentice Hall.

Mauri, Chiara (2003), "Card Loyalty. A New Emerging Issue in Grocery Retailing," *Journal of Retailing and Consumer Services*, 10 (1), 13–25.

March, James G. (1978), "Bounded Rationality, Ambiguity, and The Engineering of Choice", *The Bell Journal of Economics*, 9 (2), 587–608.

Markowitz, Harry (1952), "The Utility of Wealth," *Journal of Political Economy*, 60 (2), 151–158.

May, Kenneth O. (1954), "Intransitivity, Utility, and the Aggregation of Preference Patterns," *Econometrica*, 22 (1), 1–13.

Mazumdar, Tridib, S.P. Raj, and Indrajit Sinha (2005), "Reference Price Research: Review and Propositions," *Journal of Marketing*, 69 (4), 84–102.

Mägi, Anne W. (2003), "Share of Wallet in Retailing: The Effects of Customer Satisfaction, Loyalty Cards and Shopper Characteristics," *Journal of Retailing*, 79 (2), 97–106.

McFadden, Daniel (1973), "Conditional Logit Analysis of Qualitative Choice Behavior," in *Frontiers in Econometrics*, ed. Paul Zarembka, New York, NY: Academic Press, 105–142.

McFadden, Daniel (1986), "The Choice Theory Approach to Market Research," *Marketing Science*, 5 (4), 275–297.

Meyer-Waarden, Lars (2007), "The Effects of Loyalty Programs on Customer Lifetime Duration and Share of Wallet," *Journal of Retailing*, 83 (2), 223–236.

Meyer-Waarden, Lars (2008), "The Influence of Loyalty Programme Membership on Customer Purchase Behavior," European Journal of Marketing, 42 (1/2), 87–114.

Meyer-Waarden, Lars and Christophe Benavent (2006), "The Impact of Loyalty Programmes on Repeat Purchase Behaviour," *Journal of Marketing Management*, 22 (1/2), 61–88.

Meyer-Waarden, Lars and Chrstophe Benavent (2009), "Grocery Retail Loyalty Program Effects: Self-Selection or Purchase Behavior Change?" *Journal of the Academy of Marketing Science*, 37 (3), 345–358.

Montgomery, Henry (1983), "Decision Rules and the Search for a Dominance Structure: Towards a Process Model of Decision Making," *Advances in Psychology*, 14, 343–369.

Morewedge, Carey K., Daniel T. Gilbert, Boaz Keysar, M. Jay Berkovitz, and Timothy D.Wilson (2007), "Mispredicting the Hedonic Benefits of Segregated Gains," *Journal of Experimental Psychology: General*, 136 (4), 700–709.

Morgan, Robert M. and Shelby, D. Hunt (1994), "The Commitment-Trust Theory of Relationship Marketing," *Journal of Marketing*, 58 (3), 20–38.

Murphy, Kevin R. and Charles O. Davidshofer (1988), *Psychological Testing: Principles and Applications*, Englwood Cliffs, NJ: Prentice-Hall.

Navarick, Douglas J. and Edmund Fantino (1974), "Stochastic Transitivity and Unidimensional Behavior Theories," *Psychological Review*, 81 (5), 426–441.

Noble, Stephanie M., Carol L. Esmark, and Charles H. Noble (2014), "Accumulation Versus Instant Loyalty Programs: The Influence of Controlling Policies on Customers' Commitments," *Journal of Business Research*, 67 (3), 361–368.

Noble, Stephanie M. and Joanna Phillips (2004), "Relationship Hindrance: Why Would Consumers not Want a Relationship with a Retailer?" *Journal of Retailing*, 80 (4), 289–303.

Noordhoff, Corine , Pieter Pauwels, and Gaby Odekerken-Schröder (2004), "The Effect of Customer Card Programs: A Comparative Study in Singapore and The Netherlands," International Journal of Service Industry Management, 5 (4), 351–364.

Nunes, Joseph C. and Xavier Drèze (2006a), "The Endowed Progress Effect: How Artificial Advancement Increases Effort," *Journal of Consumer Research*, 32 (4), 504–512.

Nunes, Joseph C. and Xavier Drèze (2006b), "Your Loyalty Program is Betraying You," *Harvard Business Review*, 84 (4), 124–131.

Nunes, Joseph C. and C. Whan Park (2003), "Incommensurate Resources: Not Just More of the Same," *Journal of Marketing Research*, 40 (1), 26–38.

Nunnally, Jum C. (1978), *Psychometric Theory*, New York, NY: McGraw-Hill.

Okada, Erica Mina (2005), "Justification Effects on Consumer Choice of Hedonic and Utilitarian Goods," *Journal of Marketing Research*, 42 (1), 43–53.

O'Brien, Louise and Charles Jones (1995), "Do Rewards Really Create Loyalty?" *Harvard Business Review*, 73 (3), 75–82.

O'Malley, Lisa (1998), "Can Loyalty Schemes Really Build Loyalty?" *Marketing Intelligence and Planning*, 16 (1), 47–57.

Pacini, Rosemary and Seymour Epstein (1999), "The Interaction of Three Facets of Concrete Thinking in a Game of Chance," *Thinking & Reasoning*, 5 (4), 303–325.

Pandelaere, Mario, Barbara Briers, and Christophe Lembregts (2011), "How to Make a 29% Increase Look Bigger: The Unit Effect in Option Comparisons," *Journal of Consumer Research*, 38 (2), 308–322.

Pelham, Brett W., Tin Tin Sumatra, and Laura Myaskovsky (1994), "The Easy Path From Many To Much: The Numerosity Heuristic," Cognitive Psychology, 26 (2), 103–133.

Perdue, Barbara C. and John O. Summers (1986), "Checking the Success of Manipulations in Marketing Experiments," *Journal of Marketing Research*, 23 (4), 317–326.

Peterson, Robert A. (1995), "Relationship Marketing and the Consumer," *Journal of the Academy of Marketing Science*, 23 (4), S. 278–281.

Phillips-Melancon, Joanna, Stephanie M. Noble, and Charles H. Noble (2011), "Managing Rewards to Enhance Relational Worth," *Journal of the Academy of Marketing Science*, 39 (3), 341–362.

Podsakoff, Philip M., Scott B. MacKenzie, Jeong-Yeon Lee, and Nathan P. Podsakoff (2003), "Common Method Biases in Behavioral Research: A Critical Review of the Literature and Recommended Remedies," *Journal of Applied Psychology*, 88 (5), 879–903.

Podsakoff, Philip M. and Dennis W. Organ (1986), "Self-Reports in Organizational Research: Problems and Prospects," *Journal of Management*, 12 (4), 531–544.

Posavac, Steven S., David M. Sanbonmatsu, Frank R. Kardes, and Gavan J. Fitzsimons (2004), "The Brand Positivity Effect: When Evaluation Confers Preference," *Journal of Consumer Research*, 31 (3), 643–651.

Raghubir, Priya and Aradhna Krishna (1996), "As the Crow Flies: Bias in Consumers' Map-Based Distance Judgments," *Journal of Consumer Research*, 23 (1), 26–39.

Raghubir, Priya and Aradhna Krishna (1999), "Vital Dimensions in Volume Perception: Can the Eye Fool the Stomach?" *Journal of Marketing Research*, 36 (3), 313–326.

Raghubir, Priya and Joydeep Srivastava (2002), "Effect of Face Value on Product Valuation in Foreign Currencies," *Journal of Consumer Research*, 29 (3), 335–347.

Rayner, Sue (1996), *Customer Loyalty Schemes: Effective Implementation and Management*, Financial Times Retail and Consumer Publishing, London, UK.

Read, Daniel (2009), "Experimental Tests of Rationality," in *The Handbook of Rational and Social Choice*, eds. Paul Anand, Prasanta Pattanaik, and Clemens Puppe, Oxford, UK: Oxford University Press, 196–222.

Redelmeier, Donald A. and Eldar Shafir (1995), "Medical Decision Making in Situations That Offer Multiple Alternatives," *Journal of the American Medical Association*, 273 (4), 302–305.

Reichheld, Frederick F and W. Earl Sasser (1990), "Zero Defections: Quality Comes to Services," *Harvard Business Review*, 68 (5), 105–111.

Reichheld, Frederick F. and Thomas Teal (1996), *The Loyalty Effect: The Hidden Force Behind Growth, Profits, and Lasting Value,* Harvard Business School Press, Boston, MA.

Reinartz, Werner J. and V. Kumar (2003), "The Impact of Customer Relationship Characteristics on Profitable Lifetime Duration," *Journal of Marketing*, 67 (1), 77–99.

Ritov, Ilana and Jonathan Baron (1990), "Reluctance to Vaccinate: Omission Bias and Ambiguity," *Journal of Behavioral Decision Making*, 3 (4), 263–277.

Ritov, Ilana and Jonathan Baron (1992), "Status-Quo and Omission Biases," *Journal of Risk and Uncertainty*, 5 (1), 49–61.

Robinson, James O. (1972), *The Psychology of Visual Illusion*, London, UK: Hutchinson.

Roehm, Michelle L., Ellen Pullins, and Harper A. Roehm, Jr. (2002), "Designing Loyalty-Building Programs for Packaged Goods Brands," *Journal of Marketing Research*, 39 (2), 202–213.

Roehm, Michelle L. and Harper A. Roehm, Jr. (2011), "The Influence of Redemption Time Frame on Responses to Incentives," *Journal of the Academy of Marketing Science*, 39 (3), 363–375.

Rose, Barbara J. and Michael H. Birnbaum (1975), "Judgments of Differences and Ratios of Numerals," *Perception & Psychophysics*, 18 (3), 194–200.

Rosenbaum, Mark S., Amy L. Ostrom, and Ronald Kuntze (2005), "Loyalty Programs and a Sense of Community," *Journal of Services Marketing*, 19 (4), 222–233.

Rothschild, Michael L. and William C. Gaidis (1981), "Behavioral Learning Theory: Its Relevance to Marketing and Promotions," *Journal of Marketing*, 45 (2), 70–78.

Samuelson, William and Richard Zeckhauser (1988), "Status Quo Bias in Decision Making," *Journal of Risk and Uncertainty*, 1 (1), 7–59.

Shafir, Eldar (1993), "Choosing Versus Rejecting: Why Some Options Are Both Better and Worse Than Others," *Memory & Cognition*, 21 (4), 546–556.

Shafir, Eldar, Peter Diamond, and Amos Tversky (1997), "Money Illusion," *Quarterly Journal of Economics*, 112 (2), 341–373.

Shafir, Eldar, Itamar Simonson, and Amos Tversky (1993), "Reason-based Choice," *Cognition*, 49 (1/2), 11–36.

Sharp, Byron and Anne Sharp (1997), "Loyalty Programs and Their Impact on Repeat-Purchase Loyalty Patterns," *International Journal of Research in Marketing*, 14 (5), 473–486.

Sheth, Jagdish N. and Atul Parvatiyar (1995), "The Evolution of Relationship Marketing," *International Business Review*, 4 (4), 397–418.

Simon, Herbert A. (1955), "A Behavioral Model of Rational Choice," *Quarterly Journal of Economics*, 69 (1), 99–118.

Simon, Herbert A. (1959), "Theories of Decision-Making in Economics and Behavioral Science," *The American Economic Review*, 49 (3), 253–283.

Simonson, Itamar (1989), "Choice Based on Reasons: The Case of Attraction and Compromise Effects," *Journal of Consumer Research*, 16 (2), 158–174.

Simonson, Itamar, Ziv Carmon, and Suzanne O'Curry (1994), "Experimental Evidence on the Negative Effect of Product Features and Sales Promotions on Brand Choice," *Marketing Science*, 13 (1), 23–40.

Simonson, Itamar and Stephen M. Nowlis (2000), "The Role of Explanations and Need for Uniqueness in Consumer Decision Making: Unconventional Choices Based on Reasons," *Journal of Consumer Research*, 27 (1), 49–68.

Simonson, Itamar, Stephen M. Nowlis, and Yael Simonson (1993), "The Effect of Irrelevant Preference Arguments on Consumer Choice," *Journal of Consumer Psychology*, 2 (3), 287–306.

Simonson, Itamar and Amos Tversky (1992), "Choice in Context: Tradeoff Contrast and Extremeness Aversion," *Journal of Marketing Research*, 29 (3), 281–295.

Slovic, Paul (1975), "Choice Between Equally Valued Alternatives," *Journal of Experimental Psychology: Human Perception and Performance*, 1 (3), 280–287.

Slovic, Paul (1995), "The Construction of Preference," *American Psychologist*, 50 (5), 364–371.

Slovic, Paul and Sarah Lichtenstein (1968), "Relative Importance of Probabilities and Payoffs in Risk Taking," *Journal of Experimental Psychology*, 78 (3), 1–18.

Starmer, Chris (1999), "Cycling with Rules of Thumb: An Experimental Test for a New Form of Non-Transitive Behaviour," *Theory and Decision*, 46 (2), 139–157.

Stauss, Bernd, Maxie Schmidt, and Andreas Schoeler (2005), "Customer Frustration in Loyalty Programs," *International Journal of Service Industry Management*, 16 (3), 229–252.

Strack, Fritz and Thomas Mussweiler (1997), "Explaining the Enigmatic Anchoring Effect: Mechanisms of Selective Accessibility," *Journal of Personality and Social Psychology*, 73 (3), 437–446.

Slaughter, Jerel E., Evan F. Sinar, and Scott Highhouse (1999), "Decoy Effects and Attribute-Level Inferences," *Journal of Applied Psychology*, 84 (5), 823–828.

Smith, Andrew and Leigh Sparks (2009), "'It's Nice to Get a Wee Treat if You've Had a Bad Week': Consumer Motivations in Retail Loyalty Scheme Points Redemption," *Journal of Business Research*, 62 (5), 542–547.

Smith, Andrew, Leigh Sparks, Susan Hart, and Nikolaos Tzokas (2003), "Retail Loyalty Schemes: Results from a Consumer Diary Study," *Journal of Retailing and Consumer Services*, 10 (2), 109–119.

Soman, Dilip (1998), "The Illusion of Delayed Incentives: Evaluating Future Effort-Money Transactions," *Journal of Marketing Research*, 35 (4), 427–437.

Sopanen, Sari (1996), *Customer Loyalty Schemes in Retailing across Europe*, Oxford, UK: Oxford Institute of Retail Management.

Taylor, Gail Ayala and Scott A. Neslin (2005), "The Current and Future Sales Impact of a Retail Frequency Program," *Journal of Retailing*, 81 (4), 293–305.

Thaler, Richard (1980), "Toward a Positive Theory of Consumer Choice," *Journal of Economic Behavior & Organization*, 1 (1), 39–60.

Thaler, Richard (1985), "Mental Accounting and Consumer Choice," *Marketing Science*, 4 (3), 199–214.

Toh, Rex S, Mary-Jean Rivers, and Glenn Withiam (1991), "Frequent-Guest Programs: Do They Fly?" *The Cornell Hotel and Restaurant Administration Quarterly*, 32 (2), 46–52.

Tversky, Amos (1969), "Intransitivity of Preferences," *Psychological Review*, 76 (1), 31–48.

Tversky, Amos (1996), "Contrasting Rational and Psychological Principles of Choice," in *Wise Choices: Decisions, Games, and Negotiations*, ed. Richard Zeckhauser, Boston, MA: Harvard Business School Press, 5–21.

Tversky, Amos and Daniel Kahneman (1974), "Judgment under Uncertainty: Heuristics and Biases," *Science*, 185 (4157), 1124–1131.

Tversky, Amos and Daniel Kahneman (1981), "The Framing of Decisions and the Psychology of Choice," *Science*, 211 (4481), 453–458.

Tversky, Amos and Daniel Kahneman (1986), "Rational Choice and the Framing of Decisions," *The Journal of Business*, 59 (4), part 2, 251–278.

Tversky, Amos and Daniel Kahneman (1991), "Loss Aversion in Riskless Choice: A Reference-Dependent Model," *Quarterly Journal of Economics*, 106 (4), 1039–1061.

Tversky, Amos, Shmuel Sattath, and Paul Slovic (1988), "Contingent Weighting in Judgment and Choice," *Psychological Review*, 95 (3), 371–384.

Tversky, Amos and Eldar Shafir (1992a), "Choice Under Conflict: The Dynamics of Deferred Decision," *Psychological Science*, 3 (6), 358–361.

Tversky, Amos and Eldar Shafir (1992b), "The Disjunction Effect in Choice Under Uncertainty," *Psychological Science*, 3 (5), 305–309.

Tversky, Amos and Itamar Simonson (1993), "Context-Dependent Preferences," *Management Science*, 39 (10), 1179–1189.

Uncles, Mark D., Grahame R. Dowling, Kathy Hammond (2003), "Customer Loyalty and Customer Loyalty Programs," *Journal of Consumer Marketing*, 20 (4), 294–316.

Van Doorn, Jenny, Peter C. Verhoef, and Tammo H. A. Bijmolt (2007), "The Importance of Non-Linear Relationships Between Attitude and Behaviour in Policy Research," *Journal of Consumer Policy*, 30 (2), 75–90.

Van Heerde, Harald J. and Tammo H. A. Bijmolt (2005), "Decomposing the Promotional Revenue Bump for Loyalty Program Members Versus Nonmembers," *Journal of Marketing Research*, 42 (4), 443–457.

Van Osselaer, Stijn M. J., Joseph W. Alba, and Puneet Machanda (2004), "Irrelevant Information and Mediated Intertemporal Choice," *Journal of Consumer Psychology*, 14 (3), 257–270.

Verbeek, Marno (2012), *A Guide to Modern Econometrics*, Chichester, UK: Wiley.

Verhoef, Peter C. (2003), "Understanding the Effect of Customer Relationship Management Efforts on Customer Retention and Customer Share Development," *Journal of Marketing*, 67 (4), 30–45.

Verhoef, Peter C., Philip Hans Franses, and Janny C. Hoekstra (2001), "The Impact of Satisfaction and Payment Equity on Cross-Buying: A Dynamic Model for a Multi-Service Provider," *Journal of Retailing*, 77 (3), 359–378.

Von Neumann, John and Oskar Morgenstern (1944), *Theory of Games and Economic Behavior*, Princeton, NJ: Princeton University Press.

Von Wangenheim, Florian and Tomás Bayón (2007), "Behavioral Consequences of Overbooking Service Capacity," *Journal of Marketing*, 71 (4), 36–47.

Wansink, Brian (2003), "Developing a Cost-effective Brand Loyalty Program," *Journal of Advertising Research*, 43 (3), 301–309.

Wansink, Brian, Robert J. Kent, and Stephen J. Hoch (1998), "An Anchoring and Adjustment Model of Purchase Quantity Decisions," *Journal of Marketing Research*, 35 (1), 71–81.

Wedell, Douglas H. (1991), "Distinguishing among Models of Contextually Induced Preference Reversals," *Journal of Experimental Psychology: Learning, Memory, and Cognition*, 17 (4), 767–778.

Wendlandt, Mark and Ulf Schrader (2007), "Consumer Reactance Against Loyalty Programs," *Journal of Consumer Marketing*, 24 (5), 293–304.

Wertenbroch, Klaus, Dilip Soman, and Amitava Chattopadhyay (2007), "On the Perceived Value of Money: The Reference Dependence of Currency Numerosity Effects," *Journal of Consumer Research*, 34 (1), 1–10.

Westfall, Ralph (1962), "Psychological Factors in Predicting Product Choice," *Journal of Marketing*, 26 (2), 34–40.

Wilson, Timothy D., Christopher E. Houston, Kathryn M. Etling, and Nancy Brekke (1996), "A New Look at Anchoring Effects: Basic Anchoring and Its Antecedents," *Journal of Experimental Psychology: General*, 125 (4), 387–402.

Wirtz, Jochen, Anna S. Mattila, and May O. Lwin (2007), "How Effective Are Loyalty Reward Programs in Driving Share of Wallet?" *Journal of Service Research*, 9 (4), 327–334.

Wong, Kin F. E. and Jessica Y. Y. Kwong (2000), "Is 7300 m Equal to 7.3 km? Same Semantics but Different Anchoring Effects," *Organizational Behavior and Human Decision Processes*, 82 (2), 314–333.

Woodward, Mark (2014), *Epidemiology: Study Design and Data Analysis,* Boca Raton, FL: CRC Press.

Worthington, Steve and Alan Hallsworth (1999), "Cards in Context – The Comparative Development of Local Loyalty Schemes," *International Journal of Retail & Distribution Management*, 27 (10), 420–429.

Wright, Clair and Leigh Sparks (1999), "Loyalty Saturation in Retailing: Exploring the End of Retail Loyalty Cards?" *International Journal of Retail & Distribution Management*, 27 (10), 429–439.

Yi, Youjae and Hoseong Jeon (2003), "Effects of Loyalty Programs on Value Perception, Program Loyalty, and Brand Loyalty," *Journal of the Academy of Marketing Science*, 31 (3), 229–240.

Zeithaml, Valarie A. (1998), "Consumer Perceptions of Price, Quality, and Value: A Means-End Model and Synthesis of Evidence," Journal of Marketing, 52 (3), 2–22.

Zhang, Ying and Szu-Chi Huang (2010), "How Endowed versus Earned Progress Affects Consumer Goal Commitment and Motivation, *Journal of Consumer Research*, 37 (4), 641–654.

Zhang, Z. John, Aradhna Krishna, and Sanjay K. Dhar (2000), "The Optimal Choice of Promotional Vehicles: Front-Loaded or Rear-Loaded Incentives?" *Management Science*, 46 (3), 348–362.

Cited Websites

aa.com (2014), accessed May 7, 2014, [available at https://www.aa.com/i18n/AAdvantage/earnMiles/beyondTravel/viewall.jsp].

IHG.com (2013), "Fact sheet - IHG Rewards Club," accessed December 12, 2013, [available at http://www.ihgplc.com/files/pdf/ factsheets/factsheet_priorityclub.pdf].

InsideFlyer.com (2013), "Membership Numbers in Frequent Travel Programs," accessed December 12, 2013, [available at http://www.insideflyer.com/aboutus/press_room/facts_and_stats/current_membership.php].

Lufthansa.com (2014), accessed February 9, 2014, [available at https://www.lufthansa.com/online/myportal/lh/de/booking?l=en&cid=18002 and http://www.meilenrechner.de/spend_miles.php?language=eng].

LoyaltyPartner.com (2014), "Now also at Rewe: Collect and Redeem Payback points," Press Release, accessed February 9, 2014, [available at http://www.loyaltypartner.com/en/press/releases/announcement/article/now-also-at-rewe-collect-and-redeem-payback-points/245/.

MIX
Papier aus verantwortungsvollen Quellen
Paper from responsible sources
FSC® C105338

FSC
www.fsc.org

If you have any concerns about our products,
you can contact us on
ProductSafety@springernature.com

In case Publisher is established outside the EU,
the EU authorized representative is:
Springer Nature Customer Service Center GmbH
Europaplatz 3, 69115 Heidelberg, Germany

Printed by Libri Plureos GmbH
in Hamburg, Germany